DREAMERS

An Immigrant Generation's Fight for Their American Dream

EILEEN TRUAX

BEACON PRESS
BOSTON

BEACON PRESS
Boston, Massachusetts
www.beacon.org

Beacon Press books
are published under the auspices of
the Unitarian Universalist Association of Congregations.

18 17 16 15   8 7 6 5 4 3 2 1

This book is printed on acid-free paper that meets the uncoated paper
ANSI/NISO specifications for permanence as revised in 1992.

Text design and composition by Kim Arney

Translated by Diane Stockwell

Some names and other identifying characteristics of people mentioned
in this work have been changed to protect their identities.

Library of Congress Cataloging-in-Publication Data
Truax, Eileen.
    Dreamers : an immigrant generation's fight for their American dream /
Eileen Truax.
        pages   cm
    Includes bibliographical references.
    ISBN 978-0-8070-3033-2 (paperback)
    ISBN 978-0-8070-3032-5 (ebook)
    1. Illegal alien children—Government policy—United States. 2. Children
of illegal aliens—Education—Law and legislation—United States. 3. United
States—Emigration and immigration—Social aspects. 4. Illegal aliens—
Education (Higher)—United States. I. Title.
    JV6483.T78 2015
    325—dc23

                                                           2014031771

CONTENTS

——◆——

WE ARE ALL DREAMERS

THERE ARE ABOUT ELEVEN MILLION undocumented people living in the United States. You can't tell who they are just by looking at them, but we know they are here. As you walk down the street, ride the subway, or drive on the freeway, you may see them coming home from work, picking up their kids at school, waiting at the bus stop, cooking or cleaning rooms at five-star hotels, or even running a little business out on the corner. While it's impossible to pinpoint exactly who's undocumented and who's not by sight, we know one thing with certainty: our daily lives wouldn't be the same without them.

The work performed by undocumented immigrants is now a firmly entrenched and even essential part of the nation's economy, but attempts to resolve their status have merely turned them into political pawns. No president has dared to propose a process of massive deportation, nor has any administration openly recognized the essential role this cheap, efficient labor force plays in the national economy. Undocumented immigrants have become the political currency of private negotiations between Democrats and Republicans, legislators and government agencies, and in campaigns for office. And except for when election time rolls around and minority voters must be courted, especially Latinos, immigration reform is a hot potato no politician wants to touch.

The amnesty law passed in 1986, designed to solve the illegal immigration problem, went only halfway: it granted legal residency to three million people but didn't put effective mechanisms into place to ensure that the situation wouldn't repeat itself. It didn't establish programs to hire foreign workers in the sectors of the economy that needed them most, even though there would still be a demand for their labor. It didn't develop effective strategies to control illegal crossings along the border with Mexico. No sanctions were enacted to punish employers who hired undocumented workers, and the labor resulting from the exchange of falsified documents has become an essential moving part of the national economy's machinery.

Almost three decades later, the number of undocumented immigrants in the United States fluctuates between eleven and twelve million; six in ten are from Mexico. Many of them work in agriculture, manufacturing, construction, or the service sector. Undocumented workers make up almost 5 percent of the civilian labor force. They are men, women, and teens who came here one, two, fifteen, or twenty years ago. Sometimes they stay here for relatively short periods before returning to their countries of origin to be with their families for a while, or to try and make a go of it there. But they end up coming north again because, even though they must live in the shadows, under the constant threat of deportation, they can earn enough money here to provide the loved ones they left behind a better standard of living.

I remember a conversation I had with a woman who worked in a garment factory in Los Angeles while I was researching a story on sweatshops. The working conditions at the place were deplorable: employees worked twelve-hour shifts with no overtime pay, making seven dollars an hour, one dollar less than the official minimum wage in California at the time, in 2008. When I asked her why she put up with it, she said she had done the same work in her hometown of Puebla, Mexico, under the same or even worse conditions but had earned only fifty pesos a day, or less than five dollars. "It's the same exploitation, but here it pays better. I can support my children on what I make here," she explained.

After efforts to heighten security along the Mexican border in the wake of the 9/11 terrorist attacks in 2001, immigrants who occasionally used to return to their countries of origin stopped making those trips. The journey back was becoming increasingly dangerous and costly. The routes that undocumented immigrants had followed before, along the beaches in California or across the river in Texas, had been redirected through the deserts of Arizona and New Mexico, where organized-crime gangs were very active. Over the past decade, deaths of migrants from Mexico and Central America due to exposure and dehydration have increased in alarming numbers, as have kidnappings, extortions, and murders. Faced with this grim reality, many undocumented immigrants have chosen to take the risk just once and then pay someone to bring their family members across—women, adolescents, even small children—so they can live together permanently on this side of the border.

For the undocumented immigrants' countries of origin, the immigrants' presence in the United States has significant economic and political repercussions. For countries that heavily depend on the monies sent home, such as Mexico and El Salvador, the migration of their countrymen provides a major source of relief on two fronts: the dollars sent home help alleviate the effects of high unemployment and general lack of opportunity in the local communities. And the migrants' mere absence provides economic relief to the state, which does not have to provide basic services to the millions of citizens not residing in the country, such as public education for hundreds of thousands of school-age children, a cost now assumed by communities in the United States.

The migrants' countries of origin tend to wash their hands of whatever may happen to their citizens once they set foot on US soil, as if their own governments no longer bore any responsibility for them. Far from recognizing the double sacrifice that migrants make by taking the risk to seek out a better life and then generously supporting their communities back home, people in their countries of origin often refer to them on Internet pages or in public debates as cowards and traitors.

IN EARLY 2004, my husband and I arrived in Los Angeles with nothing more than a few suitcases and plans to make a documentary film. Like so many other foreigners living here, we told ourselves we would stay "for just a year, two at the most." Years, though, have already sped by. Other immigrants have been here for twenty or thirty years, and still others arrived just a few months ago, swearing to stay for only a little while. We have learned to smile knowingly at these new arrivals, just like the old-timers used to smile at us.

Until 2004, my personal and professional life as a journalist had unfolded in Mexico City, where I covered politics and social issues. So when after a few months in Los Angeles I started reporting for *La Opinion*—the Spanish-language daily newspaper with the largest circulation in the United States, deeply rooted in the immigrant community—I was assigned stories affecting the Mexican community in the United States, involving border-related and immigration issues.

I came across dozens of immigrants' stories; some were tales of success and triumph, others were of pain and heartbreak. And I was lucky to get to know the youngest generation of this community, children and teens whose parents had made the decision to migrate for them, bringing them to the United States. In other words, they are undocumented involuntarily, with no Social Security number or proof of residency that would make legal their presence in the country they consider their own. They are denied access to educational scholarships and financial aid, denied the opportunity to pursue a career or even land a decent job, to travel freely, or to get a driver's license. They live under the threatening shadow of deportation to a country they left as small children, a place they do not remember, where they may not even speak the language. These young people are the Dreamers, a name that comes from the Development, Relief and Education for Alien Minors (DREAM) Act, a bill introduced in the US Senate in 2001.

Over the years I've spent here, and through getting to know some of the members of this generation, I have come to realize that the only way to really understand the immigration issue is through the people who are personally affected by the policies and laws—or the lack thereof—meant to deal with the problem. Plenty of governmental agencies, universities, and nonprofit organizations perform statistical analyses, create sociodemographic profiles, and perform complex political calculations based on the undocumented immigrant population. But that's not real life. You have to step inside the lives of a few immigrants to even begin to understand their daily challenges, dramas, and accomplishments—and how they scale their own little Mount Everests even though everything is stacked against them. This perspective is impossible to imagine from inside a well-appointed office in Washington, DC. The stigma of being undocumented is deeply embedded, a heavy burden they must carry around with them every minute of every day. And for those living it through no choice of their own, life can become unbearable.

When I decided to do this book, I initially considered writing about the many reports and analyses that use statistical data to demonstrate the economic benefits of legalizing millions of undocumented immigrants and that show their potential contributions to various industries, the advantages of a diverse society, and so forth. But that would have meant providing a purely political, academic, or economic perspective, the furthest thing from the Dreamers' real, day-to-day lives. So I decided to let the Dreamers speak for themselves here and tell us about the decisions they make every day, how they have tried to form alliances, and how, faced with a lack of political will to create a legislative solution to their situation, they have decided to take up the fight for their American Dream on their own.

The ten stories in this book transcend politics and delve into the personal, showing that beyond legislative bureaucracy or immigrants' rights, the struggle of undocumented youth, the Dreamers, is fundamentally a matter of human rights. Theirs is a struggle for civil rights, for recognition of one's personal dignity, and for one's place in the world. The Dreamers' fight brings into focus the very concept of citizenship as the active exercise of rights and responsibilities in the place where one *is*, regardless of whatever some piece of paper says.

After Barack Obama's reelection in November 2012, the movement for immigration reform was once again set in motion but went nowhere. The election results proved that the Latino community's votes are critically important and cannot be ignored in the next presidential election, forcing the Republican Party, the principle opponent to a potential path to citizenship for the undocumented population, to try to build bridges into that community.

Now is the time to try and understand this community searching for its own legitimate inclusion in society, starting with the most noble and unassailable among them, the children and youth. Over the past few years, they have given the United States and the world a lesson in organization and strategy, in courage and sensitivity, that should serve as the engine of the broader immigration movement to come.

Some of their stories are told in this book. My greatest hope is that each person who reads it will understand that these young people are a part of us and that stable societies are built upon a firm foundation of solidarity and empathy. We must understand that their countries of origin are letting go of the most valuable thing they possess, their citizens—but that does not release their governments of all responsibility toward them. The young people who are blocking streets in protest across the United States fighting for their rights would otherwise have been in classrooms in Mexico, El Salvador, Guatemala, India, or Iran. Their families' situations forced them into the lives they have here now, and the very least we owe them, from both sides of the border, is an open mind. Because, one way or another, everyone who has ever migrated has been a dreamer. Because I can't imagine a better way of creating immigration policies grounded in reality than by seeing through the eyes of those fighting for their dream, committed to speaking truth to power.

CHAPTER ONE

◆

A STUDENT IN NEED

Give me your tired, your poor,
Your huddled masses yearning to breathe free,
The wretched refuse of your teeming shore.
Send these, the homeless, tempest-tossed to me,
I lift my lamp beside the golden door!

—EMMA LAZARUS, from "The New Colossus,"
a poem inscribed on the base of the Statue of Liberty

ROYCE HALL ON the University of California campus in Los Angeles was humming with excitement on the evening of December 29, 2011. Brightly lit inside, the magnificent neo-Roman building was constructed of red brick imported from Italy and modeled after the Sant'Ambrosio Basilica in Milan, and it was one of the four original campus buildings constructed in 1929. A well-heeled crowd milled around outside under the archways and passed through the tall, imposing wooden doors. Members of the academic and cultural elite enjoyed cocktails on the terrace outside the performance hall, one of the most beautiful in all of Southern California, which housed a fine pipe organ and had seen such luminaries as Albert Einstein, John F. Kennedy, Frank Sinatra, and Ella Fitzgerald, among many others, grace its stage.

That night, another bold-print name would be added to the list: the movie director and clarinetist Woody Allen would perform with his group, the New Orleans Jazz Band. After a two-hour program of music, complete with a few jokes from Allen and two encores, the well-satisfied audience left the hall and dispersed across the walkways and lawns of UCLA, which during the day serves as the setting of student life at one of the oldest, most highly regarded academic institutions on the West Coast.

The presence and participation in the UCLA community of some of the most well-known and respected names in the worlds of politics, art, and science is the school's trademark. The smallest of the ten campuses that compose the University of California, UCLA encompasses 1.7 square kilometers, which would cover about half the area of New York City's Central Park. But instead of Fifth Avenue, UCLA is just steps from legendary Sunset Boulevard in Westwood, surrounded by the tony neighborhoods of Brentwood, Bel-Air, and Beverly Hills.

Even without a sprawling campus, UCLA is the most coveted of the state universities for students of all classes who want to earn undergraduate or advanced degrees. Among its alumni, UCLA can count winners of twenty Oscars, three Pulitzer Prizes, a Pritzker Prize, and two Nobel Prizes, including the African American Ralph Bunche, who in 1950 became the first person of non-European origin to win the award, for his work mediating between Jews and Arabs in the Middle East.

The first time I strolled through UCLA's campus, I was struck by how easy it was to forget about the world beyond its borders— even the most congested highway in the United States, the 405, just a few blocks away, quickly faded from my mind. There is something about the atmosphere that seems timeless and utterly unto itself. Even though there are a few things there that remind me of "the islands" of the National Autonomous University of Mexico, or the "green corridor" of the IberoAmerican University in Mexico City, the well-manicured lawns, buildings that blend classical lines with the minimalism of the sixties and seventies, and the ethnic diversity of the students sprawled on the grass, riding bikes or walking quickly to get to class, inspire an overall feeling of peaceful well-being that is not easy to find anywhere else.

One day in 2008, a young woman originally from the Philippines pulled open one of the oversized doors of the Student Activities Center. She climbed a flight of stairs, walked through the immaculate hallways and stepped into the office of Antonio Sandoval, the director of the Community Programs Office. Standing there in front of him, she could not hold back any longer and uttered the words that so many students before her had never dared to say aloud. What she blurted would change how the UCLA community saw itself, for years to come:

"I don't have any money to eat. I don't know what I'm going to do."

AN UNREMARKABLE DOOR to a little room in the middle of a hallway opens and closes several times a day. Some people going in avert their eyes and get in and out as fast as they can, trying to pass unnoticed. Others smile at the other students, faculty, and staff they may see in the hallway. They are all members of the UCLA community, and they all understand that anyone going into that little room is not to be judged; times are hard, and solidarity and support are like a boomerang that will come back when one needs it. People leave the little room in the middle of the hallway carrying something to eat or with some food tucked away in their backpacks, hustling to get to their next class: a piece of fruit, a container of microwaveable soup, or a sandwich to get them through the afternoon. A sign on the door succinctly describes the room's function: the Food Closet.

The Food Closet is housed in the building where students can find support for and information on recreational and social activities, not necessarily related to the UCLA academic curriculum. There are student dance troupes, intramural sports teams, and Mexican American activist groups, among many others, and ample space is devoted to providing information to anyone interested in joining the military. And there is a casual dining room with microwaves, tables, and chairs, where students who bring food from home can sit down and eat.

The Food Closet is right in front of the dining area. It is the size of a walk-in closet—and many UCLA students probably have even bigger walk-in closets in their rooms at home. Inside, a refrigerator and cabinets store the donations the program receives for students who otherwise would have nothing to eat during the day. Most of the donations are packaged or canned goods, easy to open and prepare. Sometimes, food left over from catered university functions is brought here, too: trays with sandwiches that must be quickly eaten before they spoil, salads, baskets filled with fruit, chips, and cans of soda. There are paper plates, plastic utensils, cups, and napkins in the cupboards, along with packets of condiments. There are also some personal hygiene items available for the taking: deodorant, toothbrushes, bars of soap, or Band-Aids. A collage of photos of students collecting donations hangs on a wall over a table with a basket of fruit and a guest book on it.

The Food Closet was formed in 2008 and formalized in 2009 as an organization by and for students. To those living in the United States, and especially in Southern California, it can be hard to believe that a university as prestigious and world-renowned as UCLA could have students among its ranks who are hungry. In a rich country that prides itself on its generosity and ability to meet the basic needs of its people—and having enough to eat is perhaps the most basic need of all—it has come as a surprise to discover that just a few steps away from the glamour and excess of Beverly Hills, there are students struggling to scrape together enough money to pay for their tuition, textbooks, transportation, and even to support their families, with food being pushed down on their list of necessities.

While the students accepting the Food Closet's help come from diverse backgrounds, with a wide variety of reasons for finding themselves in such desperate circumstances—from a family that lost their home because they could no longer pay the mortgage, to a young man who has to help his unemployed parents—an anonymous note left in the guestbook explains why a particular group of students are the most vulnerable on the campus, at UCLA and at many other universities across the country.

> I am an undocumented transfer student to UCLA. This university has always been my dream, but being here has been one of the hardest experiences of my life. I do not receive financial aid, and I

do not meet any of the requirements to receive any kind of scholarship because I do not have a Social Security number.

These undocumented students, who are faced with serious financial challenges while going to school, who sometimes must
work full-time to pay for their studies, and who have a highly un-
certain future when they graduate, are called "Dreamers."

ON AUGUST 1, 2001, Senator Richard "Dick" Durbin, a Democrat
from Illinois, and a Republican colleague from Utah, Senator Orrin
Hatch, presented Congress with the first version of the Development, Relief, and Education for Alien Minors Act, which in the
years that followed would become widely known as The DREAM
Act. This proposal aims to help young people who were brought
to the United States as undocumented immigrants as minors and
who meet certain requirements, such as having arrived before they
were fifteen, having lived in the United States for at least five years,
and having completed two years of higher education or two years
of military service. The initiative has been presented several times
over the past decade but has not garnered the consensus necessary
for its passage into law. In 2010, the year it came closest to being
passed, it fell five votes short in the Senate.

All children in the United States, regardless of immigration
status, are entitled to a free, public education from kindergarten
through grade twelve, thanks to the Supreme Court's decision in
Plyler v. Doe in 1982. In 1975, Texas had passed a state law allowing public school districts to charge families of undocumented students tuition. In Tyler, Texas, a town about a hundred miles from
Dallas, the school district began charging a tuition of $1,000 per
year for undocumented students, under the authorization of Super-
intendent James Plyler. In cooperation with the Mexican American
Legal Defense and Educational Fund (MALDEF), a lawyer filed
suit on behalf of four families, who were allowed to remain anonymous. The Supreme Court struck down the state law and established that minors cannot be considered responsible for their own

immigration status since the decision to enter the country illegally had been made by their parents, not by the children themselves.

Even though the Supreme Court's ruling guarantees a public education through high school, it does not offer students any means to normalize their immigration status or grant them access to financial aid that would allow them to continue their studies after graduation. This legal quagmire affects more than 700,000 young undocumented immigrants over the age of eighteen and more than 900,000 minors who will transition to a kind of legal limbo once they come of age. That is exactly what the DREAM Act aims to resolve, making these legions of young people a generation of Dreamers.

WITH ALMOND-SHAPED EYES, a fine nose, and a well-groomed beard, Carlos Amador fills the room with a smile as warm as the sun. In 1999, when he was fourteen, his family arrived in Los Angeles from Mexico City. Carlos began attending high school, not speaking any English, at the age when teens are just beginning to forge their identities. He did not dare to even think about college as a possibility.

Before graduation, when he was seventeen, he had gotten his first job, cleaning a warehouse for a company that distributed food to restaurants. On the weekends Carlos worked as a watchman there and also cleaned the bathrooms and floors. Because Carlos was undocumented, he was paid a very low wage under the table, which is typical for someone in his circumstances. Being an undocumented Mexican marked him. The other workers at the warehouse treated him as if he were inferior, lacking in intelligence and dignity. They spoke to him very slowly in English, using simple words, assuming he could not understand them, even though they knew he was going to school. They often made humiliating, racist jokes around him about immigrants and Mexicans. Once, some of his white coworkers emptied a bin of trash directly onto the floor that he had just cleaned. Rushing back and forth between his job and school, Carlos attended California State University, Fullerton, where he majored in human services. It took him six years to earn a degree that usually takes four, because he could not receive any financial aid from the state and did not always have enough money to cover his expenses.

When he graduated from college, he decided to continue his studies and enrolled in UCLA's master's program in social work. Like many students, he didn't sleep much, ate when he could, and turned to the Food Closet more than once.

"It was always something we would use. I went there for myself once a week, more or less," Carlos told me recently as he looked back on his time at UCLA. "When you don't have any money left at the end of the day, you could get some instant soup there, something like that. It always helped me, and I know it has been really helpful for a lot of other students who otherwise would not have gotten the help they needed."

Over the course of his years at the university, Carlos came to spearhead the fight for undocumented students' rights, becoming a spokesperson for the movement. In July 2010, while Congress debated the DREAM Act yet again, he saw how a group of twenty-one students carried out an act of civil disobedience in Washington, DC, to put pressure on Congress. Then Carlos and eight other undocumented students in Southern California decided to carry out their own act of civil disobedience.

The next day, they began a hunger strike outside Senator Dianne Feinstein's office in Los Angeles, which they described as a nonviolent act of sacrifice inspired by the teachings of Mahatma Gandhi and the union leader Cesar Chavez. They carried out their protest at the corner of Sepulveda and Santa Monica boulevards, two of the busiest streets in the city. The hunger strike lasted for fifteen days.

"The hunger strike allowed me to think about the struggle young undocumented students must face just to survive in the United States," Carlos wrote some months later. "During the hunger strike, I talked with some people on the senator's staff, and I realized how disconnected politics are from our lives. I understood that the change that we need has to come from the people most affected by an immigration system that is broken. Our voices and our stories have to become our tools to combat this oppressive system."

While the hunger strikers camped out in front of Senator Feinstein's office, people who had heard about their struggle came to show support. Almost three hundred people came by at one time or another over the course of the fast. The protesters shared their stories with passersby, journalists, children, parents, and police officers, who would sometimes come by in the middle of the night just to see how they were doing. Strangers showed up with blankets and to offer support and encouragement. On day fifteen, a candlelight vigil marked the end of the protest, attended by community leaders and families. The hunger strike in Los Angeles was replicated in other cities across the country: fifteen students in New York fasted for ten days, three young women in North Carolina fasted for thirteen days, and the longest, carried out by the organization DREAM Act Now in San Antonio, Texas, lasted for forty-five days.

CARLOS EARNED HIS master's degree in social work. He now coordinates the Dream Resource Center at UCLA and is co-president of United We Dream, the largest organization of undocumented young people in the country. Under the slogan "Undocumented and unafraid," the group carries out public events, encouraging undocumented students to not be ashamed of their immigration status, to be proud of what they have accomplished, and to fight for their right to live in the country where they were raised, the one they think of as home.

Other organizations act in tandem with United We Dream. Some operate on a national level, such as the National Immigration Youth Alliance and DreamActivist. Others are networks of small local groups called Dream Teams, which function on the state level. Some choose names playing on the "dream" theme, such as Dreams To Be Heard at California State University, Northridge, or simple names, like Voces del Mañana (Voices of Tomorrow) at Glendale Community College in California. Parents formed Arizona Dream

Guardians in Phoenix to support their children's struggle. Several universities have active chapters of the collective IDEAS (Improving Dreams, Equality, Access, and Success) to support young un documented students who want to keep going to school.

The collective efforts of these organizations resulted in a small victory on June 15, 2012, when the Obama administration announced the measure known as Deferred Action for Childhood Arrivals (DACA), which stopped undocumented immigrants under the age of thirty-one from being deported, as long as they had no criminal record and had arrived in the United States before the age of sixteen—requirements similar to those proposed in the DREAM Act. During this reprieve, beneficiaries would receive permission to work and would be essentially exempt from deportation. This provides some relief to the Dreamers, but activists agree that they must continue their fight to see that the DREAM Act is passed into law.

"During these years I have had the opportunity to sit down at the table with state and federal legislators," Carlos told me as we talked in a conference room in the office where he now works. "I think that no matter how often we tell them our stories and try to make them sympathize with us, they don't see us as a priority. But our story shows that undocumented students have been national leaders not only in society but in politics. Sooner or later, young people are going to get the right to work. We're going to have power, and we could align ourselves with any political group, because we are the future of this country."

ANTONIO SANDOVAL'S OFFICE at UCLA directly faces the Food Closet. He has been responsible for coordinating the university's community programs for four years, and the Food Closet was started shortly after his arrival.

It was fall 2008, and many students were talking about how the financial crisis had affected them. Parents had lost jobs, and many families could no longer afford to pay the mortgages on houses they had purchased during the real estate bubble. Although I have often heard people who live outside the United States say that the United

States was not affected by the crisis—in Latin American countries, we tend to compare other countries' tragedies with our own daily struggles and we always want to be the winners—driving down the streets of Southern California at the time was heartbreaking and underscored the difference between a crisis and a recession. On a single block you might see three or four businesses that had closed their doors after many years of successful operation and houses with foreclosure signs out front, later to be auctioned off by the banks. At every socioeconomic level, the pain from what had still not been recovered in the wake of the economic collapse was palpable. If the crisis had an effect on students in general, it was clear that undocumented students had been hit particularly hard.

In the United States, every child has the right to a free education through high school. For higher education, federal and state governments provide grants and loans to eligible students to cover the cost of tuition, textbooks, supplies, and on-campus meal plans. To qualify, students must demonstrate that they are legal residents or citizens of the United States. When students lack such documentation, not only must they pay higher out-of-state tuition, but they also must come up with the money to cover all the costs associated with being a full-time college student on their own.

"So the university formed a study group to find out what our students' most pressing needs were during the financial crisis," says Antonio, his black hair framing a face with a narrow nose, glasses, and a discreet smile as we meet in his office to talk about the programs he coordinates.

A UCLA graduate with degrees in history and political science who experienced financial hardships of his own as a student, Antonio chooses his words with care and maintains his bearing as a university administrator throughout our conversation. Making it clear that the university's bylaws prohibit providing financial aid to anyone who does not qualify for it, with a gleam in his eye he tells me how he managed to put a system in place to help students who did not have enough money to buy food, without breaking any rules.

In early 2008 Antonio met with a group of students who had been researching the issue. They talked about other students who were not eating or who rummaged for leftover food in the student center. A Muslim student, Abdallah Jadallah, proposed the concept of the Food Closet to Antonio, and after sending around e-mails to some of the faculty requesting help, they received their first donations. The next steps were to find an available space, get a donated refrigerator, and spread the word about the program.

A few days later, the Filipina girl appeared in Antonio's office, saying she had no money for food and didn't know what to do. He took her to the Food Closet and told her to take whatever she needed. Unsure at first, the girl put a few things in her bag to take home.

Students in need began to spread the word and soon the program was known outside UCLA. Today, the Food Closet receives donations not only from the university community but also from people in the surrounding neighborhoods of Westwood and Brentwood, and even from as far away as Boston and New York, from individuals who were moved after finding out about struggling students who couldn't even afford to eat. The program operates under the university's honor code: take what you need; we trust you.

Although the Dreamer community at the university is familiar with the Food Closet, Antonio assures me that it is not a program for undocumented students but a program for UCLA students, period. His expression turns serious, and he gives me a pointed look, making sure this is well understood.

"I have watched an undocumented student rush in, take something, and hurry off to class, but I have also seen students from the fraternities, blonde girls, or some with their heads covered," he says. "It's hard for them to talk about food because we are in an environment where people are used to having more than enough, so students who need help pretend that they don't. And maybe someday the DREAM Act will pass and there won't be as much need among those students, but the program will still go on; there will always be somebody who needs help."

◆

MANY STUDENTS HAVE left grateful messages in the guest book on the Food Closet's table:

> "The existence of this place helps us get through the day on campus and reminds us that there is still good in the world."

> "The hardest thing is accepting the notion that there are times in life when you become dependent on the charity of others. I have worked for most of my life, over 35 hours [a week] at my community college. I have always had money problems because my family depends on my income. Because of the recession, I was unemployed for four months in the summer of 2009. I spent all of my savings paying off debts for me and my family, who also lost their jobs."

> "I am homeless right now, I sleep in my truck and I am a full-time student. If the Food Closet did not exist I would have to get by on a one-dollar Taco Bell burrito. I have no money to my name. I have no home. I am grateful to have the support of others through the Food Closet. Thank you for restoring my faith in humanity and for making it possible for me to continue my studies and achieve my dream of being the first professional in my family. Thank you."

ELIOENAI SANTOS'S FIRST memory is of himself as a little boy, crying, as an adult tries to give him a stuffed animal to soothe him. Elioenai associates this memory with coming to the United States at two years of age. Originally from Orizaba, in the eastern state of Veracruz, Mexico, his parents decided to migrate, as almost all migrants do, in search of a better future for their children. The first to make the journey was his father. Although he had wanted to be an engineer, he could not afford to go to school, and once he became a father he decided to try his luck in the United States. He arrived in California in the early 1990s and got a job working in a bodega. A few months later his wife joined him with Elioenai. Two years after they arrived, his parents gave Elioenai a little brother, a US citizen, and his mother worked taking care of other people's children as her own grew up.

Tall and slim, with fair skin, black hair, and delicate features, Elioenai has a nostalgic air about him. Without sadness or bitterness, he tells me of his early childhood, when the culture shock upon arriving in the United States gradually gave way to a dawning realization of his undocumented status and what that meant. "My parents talked about Veracruz," he says, "but I never felt like that was my place."

At home the family spoke only Spanish, so when he went to school he had to take English as a Second Language (ESL) classes. Other parents of undocumented children tried to shield them from the harsh reality of their legal status in an attempt to protect them, but when Elioenai was ten and asked his mother if he could fill out an application that required documentation he did not have, his family told him plainly of the risks he faced and what his options were. "Every undocumented person has to be prepared for the worst," his uncle told him. And "the worst" always meant being deported.

The approximately eleven million undocumented people living in the United States come from Mexico and other Latin American countries, as well as from Asia, Africa, and Europe. Undocumented people work without contracts and without worker protections, for salaries that are not always fair, at a distinct disadvantage compared with other workers, which makes them vulnerable to exploitation by their employers.

But the lack of legal residence has repercussions beyond the workplace. The life of an undocumented immigrant is affected in every facet because it must be lived in the shadows. Undocumented people cannot drive legally because they are not eligible to get a driver's license. They cannot travel freely within the country because sooner or later, they will be asked for identification that they do not have. They cannot receive most social services, because as far as the public sector in the United States is concerned, they do not exist, with one notable exception: undocumented immigrants can apply for and receive a taxpayer identification number (TIN), which allows them to submit tax returns and tax payments to the government. The Internal Revenue Service is the one federal agency that welcomes the contributions of undocumented immigrants with open arms.

In spite of these legal limitations, we know that some undocumented immigrants do drive, traveling across the country in search of work, and they do find a way to somehow receive the most basic services necessary to go about their daily lives and provide for their families as best they can. At issue is when they are identified as undocumented by the authorities and are subject to deportation. Then the life they have built over the course of one, five, ten, or twenty years goes up in smoke, becoming a dream out of reach, viewed from the other side of the border fence or from a city they had last seen years ago disappearing from view from an airplane window.

Although during his 2008 presidential campaign Barack Obama clearly stated his intention to pass comprehensive immigration reform once elected and resolve the untenable situation of millions of undocumented immigrants—including, of course, the children of those families, the Dreamers—in practice, the Obama administration has been the most brutal in recent history. Since he arrived in the White House in January 2009, on average 400,000 undocumented immigrants have been deported each year, separating families and creating a climate of deep uncertainty in immigrant communities. Although the administration maintains that most of the people who have been deported had criminal records, and that those cases are given priority in deportation proceedings, Transactional Records Access Clearinghouse (TRAC), a data-research organization at Syracuse University, found that as of 2013 less than 12 percent of those deported had any kind of criminal record.

If life is hard for undocumented families, it is even more challenging for young undocumented people who live in mixed-status homes and see how other members of their family enjoy privileges that they do not have. For example, Elioenai cannot get a driver's license, so while his friends from school or work can hop in their cars and take off on the freeways of Los Angeles, he depends on his younger brother to drive him around. Or, more often than not, he drives himself, knowing that if he gets pulled over, he runs the risk of being deported.

"The first time I got pulled over, I felt like my heart stopped," he tells me, remembering his terror. It was a sunny morning, and we had arranged to meet on one of the lawns of California State University, Northridge, where Elioenai studied journalism. The university was on break then, so the campus was practically deserted. Elioenai took me to the building that housed the offices of *El Nuevo Sol*, the Spanish-language newspaper put out by the university's journalism school and for which he served as the editor. We couldn't go into the office because the paper was closed during the break, so we went back outside and walked through the campus as he looked for a good place for us to sit down and talk. Among the many patios, outdoor tables, and benches along walkways that he could have chosen, Elioenai settled on a cement esplanade bordered by slender trees in front of Recital Hall, an imposing glass building that is home to the Valley Performing Arts Center. With our backs to the impressive theater, he told me what it's like to be undocumented, pulled over for a traffic stop, and found to be driving without a license.

"I felt like I was in a fog," he says. "I was confused, scared. The police officer asked to see my license. I said I didn't have one. He asked to see some other identification, and all I had was the matriculate [the form of identification the Mexican government administers through its consulates and embassies to Mexicans living abroad, which is accepted by US banks and agencies] from the Mexican consulate. Then he knew what was going on, and after making me sit there for a while, he asked me to call somebody who could drive the car for me.

"I was lucky that time," he goes on. "But living like that is a problem. It's a real blow to your self-esteem, because you always feel like you are somehow less. It's awful to always feel like you're inferior. You see your friends driving around, traveling to other countries, while I don't have money to go to school; I can't get any financial aid from the government. My parents support me, my friends support me, and I work, but every day is a financial struggle just to go to school.

"Sometimes people don't understand what being undocumented means," he says. "People don't know who we are, and they think of us as criminals. We are more than that. I have friends who call me 'wetback' just as a joke and say, 'Go back to your country.' But I'm twenty-two years old, and I have been here for twenty. This is my country. If I could talk to the politicians, I would say, 'Look us in the eye. We are not faceless people. We love this country.'"

Elioenai still had a year to go until graduation. I asked him what would happen after he graduated.

"I see two options," he says. "If the DREAM Act passes in the next few months, then I have a future. It's a ray of hope, and I believe in it. If it doesn't pass, then I'll have to fight for my future. It's going to take more work and it will take longer, but I'm going to do it. It's not a question of if, but when."

I developed a nice relationship with Elioenai and would talk with him every now and then, partly as a colleague and partly as a mentor. In early 2012, when I finished writing the first draft of this book, and while he was applying for Deferred Action, like most of the Dreamers were doing then, I got a message from him through Facebook, written in a mix of Spanish and English, so typical of his peers:

> Eileen, como estas? [How are you?] Tengo unas preguntas . . . [I have some questions]. Do you know of any freelance publications I can possibly contribute to? I'd rather get paid, of course, but I would just like to keep a good work flow until I get my work permit—Dios quiera [God willing].
>
> Truthfully, it's quite depressing to see everyone around apply for jobs—some have been hired already—while I have to think of the next steps.

I landed some interviews [. . .] however I wasn't chosen for the Fall PAID internships. Cositas asi me animan pero como que [Things like that get my hopes up but] they backfire because you know that you cannot get paid unless they agree to use your TIN.

Well, sorry for the rant. I just know that you understand. [. . .] Un abrazo [hug], Elioenai.

CHAPTER TWO

◆

UNDOCUMENTED AND UNAFRAID

Out of the Shadows

"MY NAME IS FERNANDA MARROQUIN. If you're watching this video it's because I was arrested in Alabama."

As she stares into the camera, Fernanda tries to look defiant. Her little-girl face tenses and she tries hard not to cry. Her jaw is set, but her big, black eyes reflect pure desperation. Originally from Peru, having lived in the United States for the past twelve years, she brushes back a wisp of her hair, which is gathered into a ponytail. She tries to keep her voice from trembling as she addresses the thousands who will see her the next day on YouTube. She says, "I am undocumented, I am unafraid, and I'm unapologetic. It's time for us to come out of the shadows."

The following night, Fernanda's video, along with those of twelve others, was uploaded and began circulating around the Internet. Each of the young people who had been arrested on the afternoon of November 15, 2011, in Montgomery, Alabama, talked for two minutes, explaining why they had taken part in an act of civil disobedience that they knew would result in their arrest. "I was born in Guanajuato, I came to this country when I was four months old, and I'm still here. Sometimes people say, 'Go back to Mexico,' but I don't even know what Mexico's like," says Krsna, an eighteen-year-old boy with a dark complexion, long, curly hair, and an ever-present smile who lives in California. In another video, Ernesto, a handsome, self-assured twenty-five-year-old with dark hair, looks directly at the camera: "I live in Los Angeles. I came here when I was a year and a half. I felt ashamed, like my friends were going to judge me because of my immigration status. But I realized that admitting that I'm undocumented and not being afraid gives you the power to help your community." "My name is Diane," a young girl in another video says, struggling to hold back tears. "I'm undocumented, and if you're watching this video, it's because I was arrested."

For anyone who's been involved with the human rights movement in the United States, civil disobedience is nothing new. At several key points in modern American history, citizens have effectively utilized nonviolent resistance to push for social change, from protests against wars and foreign occupations, to the civil rights movement led by Dr. Martin Luther King Jr., who was also very active in Alabama, to the demonstrations against globalization in Seattle, to, most recently, the Occupy Wall Street movement. But for undocumented youth, such actions could have grave consequences: those arrested could wind up not only in jail but at a border station from where they would be deported. It's not just their freedom that is at stake; it's the only life that most of them have ever known, in the country where they have grown up.

Although they are all different, the young people who have come here today to block a street in downtown Montgomery in front of the state capitol and try to get arrested have several things in common. They did not voluntarily come to the United States but were brought here when their families made the decision to come, and they are all undocumented. They have no access to a college education at a reasonable cost because they are considered foreigners, even though the government has invested in twelve years of public elementary and secondary education for them. They cannot get hired for a good, well-paying job, but they want to be productive members of the labor force in the only country they know. And even though many of them have never met before, once they decide to take part in the protests, they eventually come to know one another as well as only prisoners sharing the same jail cell can.

———◆———

THE FIRST TIME I talked to Mohammad Abdollahi, the leader of
the DreamActivist Undocumented Students Action and Resource
Network, was in Alabama, just a few days before the protest as
he prepared the handful of undocumented students from several
states who had come to participate. Mo, as his friends call him,
is a slender young man who at first glance looks older than his
twenty-six years, but watching him talk with the young protesters is enough to confirm that he is clearly one of them. His thick,
jet-black hair falls over his forehead. He has an expressive face,
with dark, melancholy eyes and heavy black eyebrows. He always
seems to be in need of a shave, with razor stubble masking acne
scars that give away his youth. When his mouth breaks into a
smile, the sadness disappears from his eyes. Although he is very
tall and gestures animatedly with his hands when he talks, Mo is
all face.

I had to go through several people before eventually getting in
direct contact with Mo. When I did, he turned out to be open and
even warm. After a few brief phone conversations, when I assured
discretion, we agreed to meet in person in Montgomery. It was
early November 2011, and DreamActivist had planned its act of
civil disobedience for midmonth. Eleven students and two parents,
all undocumented, would take part in the Alabama protest, one of
about fifteen actions that DreamActivist had organized over the
past two years.

Mo had attended every one of them: training the participants
before the event, educating them about the risks they would be
taking, and sharing stories about his work with undocumented students, a vocation that grew out of his own life experience. One day
in 2007 his mother had sat him down to have "The Talk," which
in his case, as with hundreds of thousands of other families in the
United States, was not about sex but about his status as an undocumented immigrant. This didn't especially surprise Mo. Although
it wasn't something his family often discussed, he had grown up
knowing his status and over the years had discovered the serious
limitations it placed on him. But now something new had come up:
a law known as the Dream Act was being debated in Congress, and

if it passed, Mo would have the opportunity to legalize his immigration status and continue his university studies.

"But don't look it up on the Internet, because surely the government will find out and come after you," his mother had warned. So, of course, Mo went straight to his computer and did a search for "Dream Act" on Google, and with that his life had taken a turn.

MO WAS BORN IN IRAN. When he was three years old, his father, a young mathematician, had been accepted to study at the University of Michigan. The family had moved to Ann Arbor, a city of 113,000 residents forty miles west of Detroit. After Mo's father had finished his studies and his student visa had expired, he decided to stay in the United States with his family. Mo didn't understand the full implications of his immigration status until he graduated from high school. In a city where three in ten residents are University of Michigan students, Ann Arbor's economic engine, ironically, this was the first door to slam shut. As Mo applied for college, he found out he couldn't attend because he was undocumented.

"That was when it really hit me. They reviewed my grades and said they were perfect, and they gave me an acceptance letter and a student ID number. A few minutes later, somebody came in and said, 'We're very sorry, but you didn't say you were from Iran. When you straighten out your status, then you can come back.' And they took back the acceptance letter," Mo tells me, smiling ruefully.

He first heard about the Dream Act that same year, shortly before the initiative would suffer one of its many defeats in Congress. But by then, Mo was already immersed in the issue. He had found a Myspace page where other undocumented students facing the same problems exchanged stories and offered advice on how to apply for scholarships or get a driver's license. One day, six members of the group started talking about creating a network for people who were in the same situation, and they began to organize, in spite of the fact that they were spread out all over the map, were from different countries of origin, and had never met in person.

"I think that because of some of our cultural differences, it's harder for some to stop feeling ashamed, or they feel more insecure," he says. "Those of us who have crossed that line are privileged, and we have a responsibility to work for everyone else."

That is the guiding principle behind DreamActivist: to openly recognize that their members are undocumented and invite them to come out from the shadows. The group believes that the more visible and better organized they are, the lower the risk that they will be arrested and deported. "We don't need the legislators, we need each other," Mo says. "That's the heart of it."

In 2010, once the group was established, Mo held a meeting in Minnesota with some undocumented students. When they returned to their respective states, they each got a phone call: one of their group had been detained at the airport because he didn't have an official US ID. By this point, DreamActivist had relationships with other organizations and people working for their cause in government agencies. So they got to work making phone calls, explaining that the young man who had been detained was a student, and succeeded in getting him released from custody.

"We had already been working on a number of deportation cases," Mo says, "but after that we realized we could stop deportations just by being really organized, so we thought, 'We're involved in this, we have the energy, why don't we do it on purpose?'"

And that's how Mo got the idea to organize civil disobedience protests.

LIKE MANY CITIES in the United States, Montgomery is made up of several suburban neighborhoods surrounding a downtown area that provides jobs and services for most residents. Only 4 percent of the local population is Latino. Alabama law HB 56, which was passed in June 2011 and denied basic services to undocumented immigrants and criminalized the hiring or renting of an apartment to them, effectively terrorized this small, vulnerable community. The law was a copycat but even harsher version of the Arizona law SB 1070. Under Alabama's law, elementary and secondary schools were required to report the immigration status of their students. Undocumented immigrants could be questioned, arrested, and deported at any time, and the natural reaction to this kind of persecution is to isolate oneself. People do not venture outside their homes, they stay within their own neighborhoods, and self-segregation becomes the status quo for those living with the stigma of not having a Social Security number. Some families chose to get out of Alabama and move to another state, leaving everything behind.

That is why the young Dreamers have come to Montgomery. Their theory is simple: If we hide in the shadows and stay divided, it's easier to intimidate us. If we unite, go out into the light, and demand to be treated with dignity, we can fight for our rights. This strategy has been tested before; along with the national coalition United We Dream, members of DreamActivist have carried out similar protest actions in other states, including Georgia, Arizona, and California.

My journey to Montgomery involved two flights and a three-hour drive on the highway from Atlanta. During those three hours, gazing out at the green landscape stretched along both sides of the road and very little else, I could see how hard it would be for anyone living in the area to get involved in activist organizations. Communities are very isolated and spread out, and it's practically impossible to get around if you don't have a car. Large expanses of green woods and fields can almost make you lose your sense of time and place; surely that landscape did not look any different two hundred years ago, and it may stay relatively unchanged for a hundred more. Driving down the highway with the Atlanta skyline fading into the distance in my rearview mirror, I couldn't help but think of some episodes I had seen of the zombie TV drama *The Walking Dead*, which takes place in that city. Night fell a half hour later, and I had the strange sensation that I was fleeing farther from a zombie attack with each mile southeast that I drove.

The DreamActivist group arrived in Alabama two weeks before I got there. The students had traveled from faraway states to participate—California, Illinois, Pennsylvania, Indiana—and most had driven for many hours to get there. In the days leading up to the action, they went to the neighborhoods where undocumented immigrants lived. They spent a lot of time in a trailer park, with a cluster of ramshackle mobile homes. For families who could not rent houses or apartments because they lacked the necessary documents or because they simply couldn't afford to, the trailer park was an option within reach. The dilapidated trailers, meant for temporary use, over time became a permanent neighborhood where children grow up.

I know of families who have managed to scrape together enough money to buy a trailer home—*la traila*, in Spanglish—and rent a small lot of land to install it. So they own four walls of flimsy aluminum and rent a plot of land that will never be theirs. The DreamActivists focused on the trailer park. Some of them have spent months or even years fighting for the cause in their home states, and they know from experience that it's much easier to organize people in environments that are more welcoming to immigrants than in places with few Latinos where anti-immigrant sentiment is strong. That is why they believe the work has to be done here, in Alabama.

In May 2011, at a meeting with Hispanic legislators, President Obama assured them his administration would concentrate its deportation efforts on detained immigrants with prior criminal offenses and not deport young immigrants who could benefit from the DREAM Act. The White House's announcement of this compromise reassured the DreamActivists that they would not be deported if they were arrested for engaging in acts of civil disobedience, and that prompted them to develop their current strategy.

In the days spent with the families in the trailer park, they explained to them that when people are organized, they form a network, a kind of safety net. So if you are detained, or receive an order of deportation, or are abused by the authorities based on the Alabama law, it is easier to defend yourself if other people know about what's happening, immediately react, and closely follow the situation as it unfolds. And they told them that, in their experience, when the authorities see that a community is organized, they tend to be more careful. And if the members of the community have legal advisers and know their rights, they are even more protected.

A few months earlier, Mo had been arrested along with others at a similar protest action. When they were released without charges, they were emboldened to replicate the model that Mo believes serves two functions: it helps the Dreamers to exercise and consolidate their leadership; and it sends a message to people in states with anti-immigrant laws, so they know they are not alone. The law of the strongest versus the law of dreams.

CHARISMATIC, WITH A FIRM yet friendly tone of voice, Mo knows he makes a strong leader. He tends to delegate but always maintains ultimate control. The day before the action in Montgomery he was preparing for battle, marshaling the troops. After asking me a few questions and staring intently into my eyes, he decided I could sit in on a session where the protesters would get acquainted. In these training exercises, each person shares their story, talks about their biggest concerns, and asks questions. They learn that if they are arrested during the civil disobedience action, they do run the risk of being deported. But because they are well organized and will put the media's spotlight on the situation, it will become a visible political matter. And because of that, in the end they will be released.

Even though he moves with a nervous edge and talks very fast, paradoxically, Mo never seems to be in a hurry. Putting a hand on my shoulder, he invites me to walk with him. His gaze fixed on the floor, he summarizes the DreamActivist mission as we head down a hallway in the building where the training sessions will take place, a red-brick Christian church that reminds me of the buildings the nuns would use for weekend spiritual retreats in Mexico when I was a child in Catholic school. Like those buildings, this one is practically empty and gives me the impression of a church undergoing some act of penance. Several young people involved with DreamActivist sit in a stairwell, sending text messages and talking softly. Mo talks a mile a minute, explaining the group's philosophy and strategy in an assured voice, as if he is merely pointing out the obvious.

Sitting around tables arranged in a circle in a large meeting room, the tenuous light of a rainy day filtering through the windows, the thirteen who would be participating in the civil disobedience action got ready to share their personal stories to break the ice and bring themselves closer together. In the situation they were about to put themselves in, knowing as much as they could about one another was crucial: the net that would support them over the next hours was based on trust, Mo told them repeatedly. The group's cohesiveness and ability to work together as a team would make it possible for them to emerge from the action without any trouble.

The session got under way, and people took turns talking about themselves, their experiences, and, especially, their frustrations. Catalina had made the trip all the way from Michigan. Her family came to the United States when she was just four years old. Now she is eighteen, although she looks younger: short and very slender, with a fair complexion, delicate features, and curly auburn hair. Twisting her hands nervously, looking down at the floor, her feet in sneakers crossed at her ankles, Catalina quietly tells the story of an ordinary girl whose world collapsed when she found out she had no opportunities.

"Everybody says your senior year in high school is the best, but for me it was the worst year of my life," she says. "It was time to apply to college, and I came home all excited. I sat down in my room with the application, and when I looked at what you had to fill in, I saw you had to put down your Social Security number. I cried and cried; I couldn't stop." Catalina's voice breaks, and she starts crying. "At school, all my friends talked about it, all excited. They talked about what colleges they wanted to go to, what applications they had sent already, and they asked me where I was applying. I said I hadn't decided yet."

Tears of empathy well up in the eyes of several of the others. Catalina pauses, sobbing.

"The day of my graduation, I didn't want to go because I knew they were going to announce which students were going to which colleges. When they started saying the names, something strange happened. I knew they weren't going to say my name, because I hadn't applied anywhere, but I closed my eyes and wished with all my heart they would say it. 'Please, please, please say my name.' Of course, they didn't." She pauses again, and the others wait patiently, respectfully. "I grew up thinking this was my country and I'd be a nurse someday."

Sitting across from her at the table, Belen looks at Catalina, her eyebrows raised, her expression compassionate, maternal. Like Catalina, Belen also made the fourteen-hour drive from Michigan to Montgomery. She is not a Dreamer, but her daughter Diana is. A few months earlier, Diana had been arrested and released without charges in Georgia. Knowing that Diana wanted to participate in another civil disobedience action, this time Belen decided she would be the one to take the risk. Full-figured, her eyes sadly peering from behind a pair of large, lightly tinted glasses, Belen seems happy most of the time. She doesn't speak English very well, but the passion she conveys inspires in those she talks with the patience to hear her out.

"How can we not support them, if they are being so brave? A lady I know tells me, 'We parents should be the ones getting arrested because we brought them here; it is not their fault.' And I tell her, 'Okay, then go sign up,'" Belen says, and the others in the room break into laughter. But the laughter trails off as they grow thoughtful, realizing that is the fate that awaits them in just a few hours. Until that day, the protesters getting arrested had always been students. But in Montgomery, for the first time, two parents would be among their ranks, one of them Belen. The other is Martin Unzueta, an activist from Chicago and father of Tania and Ireri, who are also members of DreamActivist.

A pervasive sense of hopelessness has marked the lives of these young people. Cynthia Perez, a chubby girl with a fair complexion and curly brown hair, is twenty-seven and came to Indianapolis from Mexico when she was twelve. Her mother had told her they were going on vacation, but after they got to the United States they never went back. Having never been consulted on this major family decision, having left without saying good-bye to her friends, Cynthia entered adolescence carrying the heavy stigma of being undocumented. Looking down at the floor, tears flowing down her cheeks, she remembers what it was like to have to deny her immigration status, every day. One day, the radio station where she worked broadcast a story on undocumented immigration. She was the one who told her coworkers, far removed from that reality, about all the challenges people living under those circumstances have to face.

"They asked me why I knew so much about it, and I admitted that I was undocumented," she says. "But we shouldn't feel ashamed because it's not our fault."

Cynthia wonders why, ten years later, anti-immigrant laws like Arizona's and Alabama's are getting passed.

"So, all the work we've been doing doesn't work? Maybe it's time to escalate and do something different."

The escalation is civil disobedience, resulting in arrest.

FOR POLITICAL ACTIVISTS, few things are more dangerous than talking to a reporter. Access to the press can ultimately determine if the action that has been carefully planned for months is a success or a failure, or results in a legal outcome diametrically opposed to the one intended. A clumsy or misinterpreted statement, an offensive or poorly chosen word could be all it takes to make a good strategy blow up.

Having worked in the field for a few years now, Mo understands this. After sitting on a tabletop in a corner of the room for the past several hours, arms crossed, staring at a fixed point on the floor, listening intently as thirteen individuals in the process of coalescing into one unified group told their stories, Mo takes over the reins in the afternoon to begin the hardest part of their training: preparing the team to confront the police, anti-immigrant spectators, the press, and, above all, their own fear.

"When you talk into a camera, you're not talking to a reporter; you're addressing everyone who will see you on television," he says. "What you say should be directed to the people of Alabama, because most of the media that's going to show up will be local.

If a reporter from a Spanish-language station interviews you, they'll probably be nicer to you. But reporters from hate radio—anti-immigrant shows have had a resurgence in the last few years, including a really popular one hosted by two guys named John and Ken—some from TV shows who don't want us here, reporters who will make direct accusations and ask incriminating questions to try to get the right sound bite for the story they want to run—what questions are they going to ask?"

The press would be notified about the event only a few hours beforehand to minimize the chance that police would find out and block access to the group. Until that moment, no one aside from the people in that room and a few others would know what was going to happen the next day.

The group started role-playing exercises, practicing answering likely questions from different kinds of reporters. When it was her turn, Belen froze. Everyone agreed that if a reporter from an English-language outlet approached her, someone else would step in to support her. The members of the group who spoke Spanish would handle the media in that language. The group spent quite a while memorizing short phrases to use in their answers that could help them avoid making a prejudicial statement. At first it was like a game as they took turns interviewing one another, but as the questions became more complicated, the mood in the room grew serious, formal, and even a little tedious.

The next step was to decide how far they were willing to go, something that only the thirteen participants who would be arrested could determine. There are three potential outcomes in civil disobedience actions. Mo carefully explained each one. Everyone in the room fixed their eyes on Mo, as in their minds they envisioned the different scenarios:

1. Try to make sure the immigration authorities do not get involved by having a strong, visible presence of immigrant-rights organizations. In this case, an arrest would remain a matter with the local police force, and anyone detained would be released after posting bond.

2. Let the arrest take its course, which could mean that ICE (Immigration and Customs Enforcement) will get involved, depending on how the local police decide to act. At some previous actions, in the interest of avoiding a media circus, the local authorities had chosen to ignore the immigration status of those arrested. This option was equivalent to leaving the outcome up to fate.

3. The protesters could openly identify themselves as undocumented immigrants by showing the arresting authorities a form of official identification from the country where they were born. The purpose would be to demonstrate to the public that the immigration authorities would not deport them, despite their undocumented status. In this case, the police would be obliged to call ICE. If ICE chose not to respond, then the local police would have to release those arrested within forty-eight hours. If the protesters arrested were called before immigration authorities, ICE could still decide not to initiate deportation proceedings against them.

Evidently, the further they decided to go, the greater the risk that they would be deported—but the stronger the message they would send. After almost an hour spent debating the pros and cons, the group decided to go with the third option. They would push it to the limit and deliberately place themselves on the brink of deportation.

"The more closely connected you are to the community, the safer you will be," Mo reminded them, validating their decision. "You will tell a different story. ICE is obviously afraid of the community, they're afraid of public opinion, of hurting their image. If they detain somebody and nobody pays any attention, nobody speaks out, that person will be deported within a few hours. But if there's a group of us and we send out an alert, we get the media involved, then people ask what's going on, and ICE doesn't want to take the risk of being scrutinized by the public.

"When people are afraid, they lose their power. We need to overcome our fear and cause a moral crisis for the Republicans.

Traditional protests are no longer enough. We have to take drastic measures."

What happened next was like a scene out of a James Bond movie or *Mission: Impossible*, where the hero explains very carefully what the plan is and what everyone has to do—failure is not an option. Mo and the other trainers who had participated in other actions gave precise instructions. Every sentence they spoke had a reason behind it and had to be followed to the letter. The plan was so minutely detailed, you could set your watch to it: they knew exactly when they would arrive at a specific location, what street they would walk down, where they would be stopped, and even toward which side of the street they should be looking. Seemingly unimportant details like what they would be wearing or how they should get up while they were being arrested could mean the difference between getting released or getting into serious trouble. That day, I learned exactly how one should go to jail peacefully during a civil disobedience action.

First, if a protester wants to be arrested, then the goal is that the charges brought be for a minor offense, not for a felony or anything serious. It's important that no police officers get hurt in any way during the action, and there must be no damage to public property. No resistance should be put up whatsoever, and the person being arrested should not do anything that could be interpreted as "disturbing the peace," the most likely charge to be brought.

Next, when the detainees arrive at the jail, men and women will be separated, and they will spend most of their time there sitting in plastic chairs. They will probably be cold, because the blankets in jail are very thin. They might want to put their arms around one another just to stay warm, but touching is strictly prohibited. They are not allowed to talk, either. Detainees are allowed to wear only one article of clothing above the torso, so they should make sure they dress in long sleeves. The best thing to wear from the waist down is a comfortable pair of jeans, and detainees should also be sure to wear socks, since sandals or open-toed shoes will be taken away. If women are wearing bras, they should be wireless, because wires of any kind are not allowed inside jails or detention areas for security reasons.

Once the organizers had explained all of this, one of them passed around a list to make note of who needed a long-sleeve shirt, jeans, a pair of socks, or a wireless bra. Someone would go out and purchase those items for them first thing the next morning.

The last part of the training was an exercise simulating an arrest. Now it was dark outside, and everyone was getting a bit tired. But the thirteen participants sat down on the ground, just as they would the following day to block the street. A heavy-set young man from the organization played the role of an arresting police officer. He roughly brought each of the thirteen to their feet, one at a time, loudly barking orders at them:

"Get up! *Get up!* Spread your legs!"

Of course it was just a simulation, but everyone in the room looks on silently and wide-eyed as the make-believe police officer gets Cynthia to her feet and gruffly puts her hands in handcuffs behind her body. After putting the handcuffs on, he puts her face against the wall and uses his foot to kick her feet out, separating her legs. I feel a shiver up my spine, that paralyzing feeling of dread you get while watching violence being inflicted on someone else but not wanting to risk getting hurt yourself. Cynthia doesn't resist but starts to cry. A sad hush falls over the room until Mo says the exercise is done. The big "police officer" removes Cynthia's handcuffs as gently as he can and apologizes to her. Mo points out that in real life no one would offer them any kind of apology, ever.

As the other protesters take their turns, the group decides on what slogans to shout at the protest the following day. They will start with "No courage, no change" and "No justice, no peace."

Mo reminds them that they should always be friendly and courteous toward the police: "You can't treat them the way they're treating us—just the opposite," he says. "You have to kill them with kindness. While they are arresting you, make the experience as personal as you can for that officer. This is a chance to be face-to-face with authority; talk to them straight from your heart. That same officer might arrest somebody else the next day. How they treat that person the next day could depend on how you act. And while they're arresting you, hold your head high, because the media will be there. Do you want to look ashamed or proud?"

The final instruction of the day is about a telephone hotline put in place and available to them around the clock. Right before they get arrested, they will write the hotline number down in marker on their left arms so they will always have it with them. While they are being transported to the police station, they can communicate through text messages with the organizations supporting them. "You all know the plan, and we do too," Mo says. "We have to trust each other."

MOTELS IN AMERICA are practically all the same, no matter where they are: ugly buildings, rows of doors that seem too small leading into rooms that are just that and nothing more, the best you will get for the price. The cheapest are always on the outskirts of town, usually right next to the highway so that the roar of traffic is heard all night through the thin windows. But if you try, you can imagine it's the roar of the ocean, and it could even become a soothing sound to get you to sleep.

The DreamActivists stayed in this sort of motel in the outer reaches of Montgomery. The parking lot, a flat sheet of asphalt in front of a row of identical doors, became an extension of their headquarters for three days. The morning of November 15 passed slowly for everyone. By noon, a heavy heat filled the motel rooms, the parking lot, and seemingly everywhere. The DreamActivists were four to a room: towels, clothes, empty pizza boxes, water bottles, and a few cans of beer were piled on top of the few pieces of motel furniture, a reminder that the people staying there were barely more than kids, poised on the brink of adulthood. As one o'clock approached, they all checked their watches, looked around at one another, and got into cars for the ride over. The press had been invited to come at two. Each protester was fully prepared to be arrested, searched, handcuffed, questioned, taken to jail, and locked up in a cell.

People had started to gather around the capitol building in the heart of downtown Montgomery. A steamy heat very typical of the South rose in the air, the kind that makes your clothes stick to your body. The lush green lawns surrounding the municipal buildings already bore the marks left by curious onlookers: little holes in the grass from the high-heel pumps worn by reporters in tight skirts, pacing around, trying to get an interview with one of the protesters. There were holes left by television camera tripods and footprints of the young people ready to take videos of their friends on their cell phones to be uploaded to Facebook, YouTube, and Twitter so the world would know that on that day in Alabama, thirteen undocumented people sat in the middle of the street blocking traffic, knowing that they would be arrested but that they were unafraid.

Alabama's capitol building is like most in the United States: an immaculate white dome over stately columns along the entrance, surrounded by carefully manicured lawns and sidewalks that are not very crowded on a typical weekday. Suddenly, at the agreed-upon hour, a rising murmur outside prompted workers in the government offices to go to their windows and see what was going on. They saw an incredible sight: a line of students wearing black T-shirts, fists raised high in the air, marching through the city streets. The first chants began: "Undocumented and unafraid, undocumented and unafraid!" Behind them marched a group of about fifty people, many of them mothers and children from the trailer park, carrying signs they had made to support the protesters: "Don't separate families." "We want an Alabama without fear." "Governor Bentley, stop attacking my family."

Four of the protesters calmly planted themselves in the capitol building's entryway. Seated in a circle in front of the metal detectors at the entrance, they declared they would stay right there until the governor agreed to meet with them. "But the governor's not here," a harried receptionist told them. "That's all right, we'll wait," one of the protesters responded. Her eyes wide, an African American reporter asked them how long they planned on staying there.

"Until Alabama stops enforcing these racist laws."

The reporter looked back at her cameraman with an expression of disbelief, trying to understand the logic behind this seemingly irrational position. I pictured her telling the story to her friends later, still puzzled. Maybe someone would then explain to her that was exactly what civil disobedience was.

"But laws can't be changed in one or two days," she said. "You can't stay here that whole time."

"Yes I can," said a protester. "We're going to stay right here."

While this was going on inside the capitol building, outside, on Washington Avenue, the rest of the group spread a large black blanket out over the street, with a slogan printed on it reading, "We won't stay in the shadows." Then they sat down on it, blocking traffic.

The police arrived a few minutes later, blocking off adjoining streets with patrol cars and patrolling the area while talking into walkie-talkies. Passersby who stopped to watch what was going on could hardly believe what they were witnessing, something that had not happened in Alabama in recent years: a group of young people deliberately trying to get arrested, as the police called for reinforcements. The bravery of another can often counteract our own apathy. A few minutes later, people gathered around, shouted encouragement, and applauded the protesters. Nico, one of the student protesters, stood and addressed the growing crowd through a megaphone. "We have been here protesting for an hour and the police haven't arrested us. If this were a raid, they would have arrested us by now. This shows that when the people are organized, they can't hurt us. Not having papers does not mean you have no rights."

Although the day before Mo had kept a relatively low profile, on the day of the protest he was a highly visible, rock-star presence, a messiah for the cause. He closely supervised all the details of the protest, greeting sympathizers, giving instructions to volunteers, watching out for the arrival of the police, talking to the media. The quiet, almost childlike Mo of the night before was now a leader who talked with the police force's negotiator. At times he was surrounded by microphones and television cameras.

His carefully worded comments, structured in short phrases to provide the media with the sound bites they needed, would play perfectly on television.

Several police officers exchanged looks and awaited instructions. An African American officer wearing a rain jacket issued an alert: the protesters had fifteen minutes to get off the street or they would be forcibly removed. Another African American officer who spoke Spanish repeated the message in that language. Not a minute had passed before it started to rain, right on cue, like a scene out of a movie. Big raindrops pelted the police, the protesters and their families, the stunned residents of Montgomery, and the even-more-stunned members of the press. The rain soaked the protesters, their blanket on the street, and the handmade signs held up by children standing on the lawn. The rain eclipsed the arrival of a yellow bus that looked like an elementary-school bus but which was used to transport people in police custody. The rain signaled the start of the arrests.

Diana went over to her mother and hugged her tightly. Belen whispered in her daughter's ear, the rain serving as the perfect backdrop for their teary good-bye. The support team for the protesters rewrote the hotline number, which had been blurred by the rain, on their arms. Family members and friends hurried to offer their last hugs and words of encouragement to the Alabama 13, until a police officer stepped into the street.

"Please stand up."

"Am I under arrest?"

"You're under arrest."

Their hands bound with plastic rather than metal handcuffs, in front of their bodies rather than behind, the arrest procedure was somewhat less brutal than what they had anticipated and trained for the day before. One by one, the protesters were escorted onto the bus, and once seated inside, they held their hands up to the windows, waving good-bye. Myasha, an angelic-looking, slender eighteen-year-old, easily rose to her feet when two officers ordered her to stand, her long, straight, black hair dripping wet. She stared sadly down at the ground as she was handcuffed. The two officers led her to the bus, one on each side. Suddenly, she seemed to re-member one of the instructions from the night before. Still walking, she straightened up as tall as she could, held her head high in the air, and shouted through the rain, "Undocumented and unafraid!"

The arrests of the Alabama 13 ended at five o'clock that eve-ning. Taken to a detention center in Montgomery, they remained in jail for two days while their supporters raised money for their bonds, three hundred dollars each. They were charged with disturb-ing the peace, but even though they all openly admitted they were undocumented, not one was placed under ICE jurisdiction. Hours later, they found out that Todd Strange, the mayor of Montgomery, had made sure the matter would not attract any further scrutiny by talking with immigration authorities in Washington. The mayor assured them that the protesters had not provided them with correct information and, according to records that the mayor had person-ally reviewed, that all thirteen were in the country legally.

A picture of the thirteen standing outside police headquarters in Montgomery, their fists raised high, smiling broadly, ran in all the newspapers that day and on the television news. Even the fam-ilies in the trailer park saw it.

CHAPTER THREE

—◆—

DREAM SELLER

RICHARD "DICK" DURBIN looks like a stereotypical image of an insurance salesman. He's about average height, soft-spoken with an unimposing build. But he somehow comes across as so trustworthy that you'd buy whatever it was he happened to be selling. Of all the careers he could have chosen that would make good use of his image as a man you can trust, he opted for politics. The senator from Illinois is sixty-nine, with fair skin, gray hair, and an affable smile. The signs of aging that inevitably come with the passage of decades in his case are most noticeable in the laugh lines around his eyes and mouth, making me think he has spent much more time smiling than frowning. When he's serious, the lines that appear on his forehead lend him an air of studious concentration. He favors dark suits with red or blue ties. He has an easygoing way about him, as if he is never in a rush. He seems just as at home on the Senate floor, where he has served for the past seventeen years, as he does at a press conference with teams of reporters and cameras swarming around him.

On September 20, 2011, Durbin stood on the blue carpet during a Senate session, holding a large photograph of a young girl. He faced his colleagues in Congress and for the umpteenth time told them how vitally important it was that they pass the DREAM Act. Wearing a gray suit, a white shirt, and a blue tie that matched the carpet he stood on, this consummate salesman settled in to once more deliver the pitch for the one deal he has not been able to close.

"Ten years ago I presented the DREAM Act, an important bill for thousands of people in the United States who literally live with no status, without a country," he said. "The DREAM Act says that if you came to this country as a minor, if you have lived in the United States for a long time, if you are of good moral character, if you graduated high school, if you are willing to finish two years of college or to serve for two years in the military, then you will have the opportunity to legalize your status in the United States. The young people who it would benefit—for many have never known any other country in their life—they go to school, pledge allegiance to the only flag they know, sing the only national anthem they know, speak English, and still have no future in the United States because they don't have a country. Because their parents brought them here as children without the necessary papers, they have no country, and no future. The DREAM Act would give them the chance to succeed and show that they can make this a better nation."

Durbin held up a photograph of a young woman from India, with long black hair, dark skin, thick eyebrows, big, round eyes, and a bright smile. Her image filled up the room, and the senator told her story.

MANDEEP CHAHAL ARRIVED in the United States from India when she was six years old. Now she is twenty-one and has always lived in the San Francisco Bay Area in California. She's an excellent student, enrolled at the University of California, Davis, where she has focused on neurology, physiology, and behavioral studies, hoping to be a doctor one day. She is also committed to public service and to volunteering in the community. When she was in high school, Mandeep helped to found an organization called A Dollar for Life, which aimed to alleviate poverty. When her class cast their votes for the student "most likely to save the world," Mandeep was the clear winner. Once she started college, she joined the antigenocide organization STAND and soon became its co-president.

In spite of her enormous potential, a process of deportation was initiated for Mandeep and the rest of her family in 2010. Her reaction and those of dozens of her friends circulated in the most natural way their generation knew: on Facebook. They described her case and asked for help, and the response was overwhelming: almost twenty thousand people sent messages to the Department of Homeland Security requesting that her deportation be stopped. On the day she was supposed to leave the country, Mandeep and her family received a reprieve, allowing them to remain in the United States for one more year. Then Mandeep wrote a letter to Senator Durbin:

> I have lived in the United States for fifteen years, and I consider it my home. My family, my friends, and my future are in the United States, the place where I belong. My dream is to be a pediatrician, to help the most innocent and defenseless among us. I hope to serve low-income communities who otherwise could not afford medical attention. I want to stay in the United States to keep making a difference, and to give back to my community part of all it has given to me.

In a 2012 interview with *Time*, Mandeep was asked why she wanted to become a United States citizen. She replied simply, "Because I am American."

I MET STEVEN CAMAROTA in Washington, DC, in July 2010, while I was attending the Scripps Howard program on immigration held at the International Center for Journalists. The ten participants were all reporters actively covering issues relating to immigration. One of the program's objectives was to facilitate a direct dialogue with the principal actors on the issue in the political world. Analysts—directors of organizations both for and against immigration reform that could legalize the status of the approximately eleven million undocumented immigrants in the country—came to talk to us, laying out their arguments and answering our questions. Camarota came to one of these afternoon sessions, and the reporters steeled themselves for battle.

Steven Camarota has been a constant figure in debates over the DREAM Act because of his role as director of research at the Center for Immigration Studies (CIS), a nonprofit organization that aims to present information on the social, economic, environmental, and security costs of illegal immigration. Making clever use of numbers and statistics, Camarota has become an expert in formulating arguments against legalizing undocumented immigrants. Heavyset, with a round face, short brown hair, and friendly expression, wearing metal-framed glasses and a tie that at times seems to be squeezing his neck a little too tightly, he likes to adopt a television-anchorman voice when he animatedly explains his views to Congress. He always frames his arguments as purely objective analyses of the facts, a stance that pro-immigration groups call into question because of some CIS members' links to far-right and even white supremacist groups.

Camarota asserts that of the total number of possible beneficiaries of the DREAM Act—around 1.6 million by some group's estimates, or 2 million, according to CIS—around half of them would enroll in college. This would cost American taxpayers $12 billion, by his calculations. And although figures released by Congress estimate that within ten years, $23 billion would be pumped into the economy thanks to the inclusion of the Dreamers in the labor market—which, of course, would make legalizing their status a very wise investment for the country—Camarota argues this figure is wrong because the DREAM Act would require young people to attend just two years of college, not the four years necessary to graduate with a bachelor's degree, and having that degree is what makes a real difference in terms of earnings.

"Maybe some of them would graduate, but the reality is many of these young people come from low-income families and they are going to have to start working as soon as possible, so they would not go to school for four years," Camarota explained to us that afternoon in Washington. "There are studies that show [that] someone who only has one or two years of higher education, but didn't earn a degree after four years, does not earn any more than a high school graduate."

Those who are knowledgeable about issues surrounding immigration question the slant of Camarota's positions. He assumes that the financial and even cultural limitations of undocumented immigrants make it virtually impossible for them to ever make a meaningful contribution to this country's productivity. For instance, at one point in our session with him, he brought up the pregnancy rate of Latina teens. Trying to motivate teens to be good students using economic arguments was, in his words, "stupid; it's just public relations. And for them it's not fair; it's unreasonable, because there will always be someone whose inclination would not be to go to college."

The journalists' session with Camarota was not especially productive, with people on opposite sides of the issue mostly talking past one another. The reporters all had access to figures and statistics from other groups that discredit CIS, an organization not considered legitimate by some politicians. By the end of the two-hour meeting, Camarota was still unable to come up with any solid data to support his view that poverty levels among the Dreamers would keep them from being full-time students, even if they did receive financial aid. Still, one of the points he made that afternoon came back to me a year later, at the civil disobedience action organized by DreamActivist in Alabama.

It was a Monday morning, and the DreamActivists were having breakfast at an IHOP before going to their all day training session in preparation for the following day's protest in downtown Montgomery. They sat around tables with plates piled high with pancakes and maple syrup; the clattering of coffee cups and their conversations in Spanish and English filled a whole side of the large restaurant. Among them was Fernanda, the young girl born in Peru with smooth black hair and black eyes. She would be arrested the next day, along with twelve others.

The young men and women, representing different states and different levels of engagement in the Dreamer movement, exchanged views animatedly. Being undocumented in California, where one-third of the population is Hispanic and where there are more than thirty "sanctuary" cities for immigrants, is very different from being undocumented in Arizona, where harassment and persecution are a part of daily life. Not surprisingly, the ones advocating the most radical positions in terms of resistance and protest came from states where undocumented communities feel the most protected and the least threatened.

"Well, I am undocumented but not a Dreamer," Fernanda, who lives in Pennsylvania, said as she poured herself another cup of coffee. "That law doesn't define me. The way it's written implies that I don't deserve to benefit from it, because I wasn't a good student in high school. I didn't like school, so I would cut class, go out drinking, all kinds of stuff. I'm not the model student they want."

Fernanda was referring to the requirements established in the DREAM Act for young undocumented people to legalize their status. They would have to be enrolled in college for two years or serve in the military for two years and have "good moral character," whatever that means. The bill also stipulates that anyone with prior criminal arrests would not be eligible. If all of the requirements are met, then there are three stages: first, a conditional, temporary residency is granted for six years, followed by permanent residency, and then the possibility of applying for citizenship after five more years—almost twelve years to finally get the piece of paper that says this is your country.

"Life is more complicated than that," Fernanda said. "We're like any teenager, any young person. We make mistakes. We're not perfect. They didn't have to ask us to be perfect as a condition to giving us a right. That's why I'd rather say I'm fighting for all immigrants."

Cesar, a young man with light hair, small eyes, and a mischievous expression, is Fernanda's younger brother—he's twenty-one and she's twenty-two. He also came to this country twelve years ago, with their parents. When his parents lost their family business in Peru, they were no longer able to send their children to school, so they decided to emigrate to the United States. Cesar agreed with his sister about the DREAM Act's limitations. What if somebody wanted to be an artist, like he does? You don't necessarily have to go to college for that.

I remembered Camarota's arguments, and it seemed to me that, at least in one aspect, he might actually have a point. His way of explaining his theory that undocumented young people would not earn a four-year degree seemed overly simplistic and without basis. But it's possible that the statistics are not as rosy as the pro-immigrant organizations present. Not everyone who would be eligible to try to legalize their status under the DREAM Act would meet all of the requirements—enrolling in college or serving in the military and being of good moral character—and it's possible that some would attend college for two years as required only to become legal, not out of any genuine desire to earn a degree.

"Sometimes you graduate high school and you don't want to go to school right away. You don't always know what you want to do," Cesar went on. "Because of that you don't deserve to have legal status? You could still contribute to your country doing other things, like lots of people do, right? We don't want to be defined by politics, that's not who we are. You don't have to be perfect; you just have to be a person, that's all."

When the two siblings had stopped talking, all of the tables around them had fallen silent, and several of their companions nodded their heads in agreement.

THE PRACTICE OF BRINGING a large photograph with him onto the Senate floor has become routine for Dick Durbin. In recent years, he has told the stories of more than fifty Dreamers to his colleagues, trying to put a face on his legislative initiative, which has languished in Congress for the entire new millennium. Speaking calmly, he displays a giant picture of a beaming Latina girl, wearing glasses and dressed in her graduation cap and gown. He insists on telling her story.

Fanny Martinez was brought to this country from Mexico when she was thirteen. Her family settled in Addison, Illinois, where she graduated from high school with excellent grades. In 2010 Fanny graduated summa cum laude with a degree in sociology from Dominican University in River Forest, Illinois. She decided to pursue a master's degree at the University of Chicago's Harris School of Public Policy.

Fanny is married to David Martinez, an American who has served in the military for eight years. On the day that Senator

Durbin told Fanny's story at a Senate session, David was on a mission in Afghanistan. "While David is defending our country, his wife could be deported," Durbin emphasized.

Fanny and David's case is not unusual. The immigration system in the United States is one of the most inefficient on the planet. Proof of this is the enormous backlog and delay in family petitions filed by citizens or permanent residents. In some cases, even though there may be a way for a person to legalize their status, the glacial slowness of the filing process and the very high demand make it virtually impossible for the petition to ever be formally granted. A recent report from the National Immigration Forum indicates that if a citizen files a petition for his wife or an underage child, the case will take several months. But if a legal resident files—and this is the case for a large number of immigrants who have a green card but not a certificate of naturalization—the same process will take at least two and a half years. If the child is over twenty-one, the wait extends to seven years, and if the petition is filed for a sibling, it can take as long as eleven and a half years.

If these figures published by organizations that analyze data from their offices sound alarming, the anguish they cause in the real world is even greater. At Dreamer protests, there's always somebody yelling that the protesters should go to "the back of the line," along with the thousands of foreigners who are trying to legally immigrate to the United States. But that line is not a real option. Some young adults whose parents are now legal residents have told me that their family petitions have been in process for ten, fifteen, even eighteen years, and they are still not close to a ruling. In 2012, immigration authorities were tackling family petitions filed in 1996.

Fanny's case is trapped in this bottleneck.

"My husband is always so worried about my situation. He knows I am always at risk of deportation, and he's afraid that when he gets back from Afghanistan I won't be here anymore," Fanny wrote to Senator Durbin. "Passing the DREAM Act would let me live without fear and frustration, and it would let my husband plan our future without the shadow of my possible deportation or lack of opportunities hanging over us. I care about my community, and I know if I am granted legal residency in the United States, I can help to build a better society."

ON SATURDAY, MAY 15, 2010, on a highway in Maine, a pickup truck collided head-on with a car. Two days later, an auditorium on the UCLA campus filled with hundreds of students and friends of Tam Tran and her best friend, Cynthia Felix, both Dreamers, who had been riding in the car and had lost their lives. Tam and Cynthia left a mark on an entire generation of Dreamers who remember them as pioneers in the struggle for undocumented immigrants' access to higher education, and for the DREAM Act's passage.

When I started thinking about writing a book about the Dreamers, I gathered some of the stories I had covered over the course of my work as a reporter and some I had read about over the years in other media. Of all of those stories, I think the one the *Los Angeles Times* published on Tam in 2007 affected me the most deeply because so many things about it were absurd and senseless.

Tam Ngoc Tran was born on October 30, 1982, in a refugee camp in Germany. Like thousands of others, her parents had fled Vietnam, escaping by boat after the fall of Saigon in 1975. Unlike most refugees, who were picked up by American boats, the Trans were rescued by the German navy. In Vietnam, Tam's mother had left school to work as a street vendor and make money for her family. Her father had been a little more fortunate and was a university student.

After being rescued on the high seas, the Trans lived in Germany as refugees. Tam was born there, and later she was joined by her younger brother, Thian. When Tam was six years old, her parents decided to move to the United States to reunite with the rest of their family, who had settled in California. They figured that, after all, "this was America" and there would be a place for them there somehow.

Once they were in the United States, Tam's parents filed a petition for political asylum, arguing that returning to communist

Vietnam would be too risky for them. They were confident that the US justice system would sympathize with their plight. After several years, they were informed that their petition had been denied, because they had emigrated from Germany, not directly from Vietnam. An immigration court ordered that they be deported to Germany. But when they met with officials at the German consulate, they were told that Germany would not accept them because they had not been born there. They also found out that Germany does not guarantee citizenship to those born under refugee status within its borders. So despite the fact that Tam had been born in Germany, she was not considered German because she had been born to citizens of Vietnam, a place she had never been. Even after the United States issued an order of deportation against her, neither Germany nor Vietnam would accept her. Like some plot out of a movie that could only be satire, Tam became a person without a country.

She graduated from UCLA with honors with a master's degree in American literature and was immediately hired by the university to work full time as a videographer; she was also accepted into UCLA's doctoral program in cultural studies. Although Tam won two scholarships for her doctoral studies, it wasn't enough to cover the $50,000-per-year tuition. Like all undocumented students, Tam was ineligible for federal aid, so she could not enter the program. She started saving money, working various jobs so she could realize her dream, but because of her immigration status, the work permission granted by the government had to be renewed annually, and that never happened on time. Tam got used to losing her job every May as she waited for the new work authorization to come through. When Tam died, she was working toward her doctorate in American civilization at Brown University. She used to joke about it, saying that if she became an expert on America, then they would have to give her citizenship. Tam's dream was to continue doing academic research and to make films on social issues.

On May 18, 2007, three years before her death, Tam testified in Congress as part of the hearings on the DREAM Act that were held that year—one of the many times that Senator Durbin and other members of Congress have tried to get the law passed. Tam testified:

> I hate filling out forms, especially the ones where I have to check off boxes of categories I don't identify with. Place of birth? Germany. But I'm not German. Ethnicity? I am Vietnamese, but I have never been to Vietnam. But these forms never ask me where I grew up or went to school. . . . When I get to a question asking about my citizenship, I rebelliously check the box that says "other" and write in "the world." But the truth is I am culturally American, and specifically I consider myself Southern Californian. I grew up watching *Speed Racer* and *Mighty Mouse* every Saturday morning. But as of now my national identity is not American, and even though I cannot be removed from United States territory, I cannot become a citizen of this country until the law changes.

That day in the congressional hearing Tam talked about her own case, patently absurd no matter how you looked at it. She also talked about the relatively privileged position she was in, because she could use her work authorization as a form of ID that would allow her to fly to Washington and enter a federal building to give her testimony.

"Without the DREAM Act, I have no chance of getting out of the immigration limbo I'm in. I will always be a perpetual foreigner in a country I've always felt I belonged in," Tam told the members of Congress, who have listened to these Dreamers' speeches again and again and again. "For many of my friends, graduation is not a rite of passage to becoming a responsible adult. Instead, it's the last time they can feel like they belong to something like Americans do. As students of an American college, my friends feel like they are a part of an American community, they feel like they are living the American Dream, among people who are their equals. But after graduation, they will be left behind by their American friends, with no chance of getting a job that would make use of the degree they have just earned. My friends will become just another undocumented immigrant."

In October 2012, the Center for American Progress (CAP), a nongovernmental organization, released data supporting the premise that the DREAM Act would not only benefit young undocumented immigrants themselves but would also be a wise investment for the country as a whole. The report's findings circulated widely, prompting those for and against the DREAM Act to respond, filling up blogs and social media with discussion. CAP projected that there could be around 2.1 million young people eligible to benefit from the DREAM Act immediately or within the next couple of years, a figure very similar to Camarota's number. But Camarota would never acknowledge any of the other findings in the report: that the act's passage would mean an infusion of $329 billion into the US economy and create 1.4 million new jobs by the year 2030, with a $10 billion increase in federal tax revenue.

Given that the Dreamers are unevenly distributed throughout the country, some states stand to benefit more than others. For example, California has the largest number of potential beneficiaries of the act, with more than 500,000 Dreamers. That state could see an increase of $100 billion in economic activity, while Texas could see a gain of more than $66 billion. Even in states with relatively few Dreamers, passage of the law would still have a positive impact. Maryland is home to only 36,000 Dreamers, yet the state would see a gain of $5 billion in economic activity, enough to help create 19,000 new jobs. According to the report, there is not a single state that would not benefit from the DREAM Act's passage.

CAP released its report to coincide with the Obama administration's announcement of the Deferred Action for Childhood Arrivals (DACA) program. Although this measure does provide relief for a period of two years for almost 1.4 million who qualify, it does not offer a permanent solution to their nebulous immigration status. As far as citizenship goes, according to Senator Durbin they will all still be young people "without a country."

THE FULL NAME of the city of Los Angeles has always sounded like a poem to me. El Pueblo de Nuestra Señora la Reina de los Angeles del Rio de Porciuncula was the second town founded by the Spanish during their colonization of Alta California in 1781, after San Diego. El Pueblo, as the cluster of brick and adobe buildings that was the heart of the city in that era is known today, is centered around a plaza with a bandstand at the center; Olvera Street is the main thoroughfare. There are twenty-seven historical buildings in the zone, as well as a Catholic church, Nuestra Señora Reina de Los Angeles. Because it so closely resembles a stereotypical Mexican town's central plaza— townspeople out for a leisurely stroll on the weekends, street musicians performing, balloons and handcrafts for sale at little stands—this area is known as Placita Olvera, and the church is called *la iglesia de La Placita* ("La Placita's church").

Aside from its religious significance, La Placita has historically been very closely tied to the immigrant community of Los Angeles. In 1910, Pope Pius X guaranteed all Mexicans the right to marry, be baptized, and take part in other religious services at La Placita, because it was so difficult for them to find acceptance at other churches in the city due to discrimination or a lack of proficiency in English. In the 1980s, when a wave of refugees fleeing the civil war in El Salvador began arriving in Los Angeles, La Placita was the first Catholic church to declare itself a sanctuary for immigrants. Under Father Luis Olivares's leadership, the church sheltered about two hundred people at night, defying the government's ban on providing asylum to undocumented immigrants.

The sanctuary theme was renewed after anti-immigrant measures were put into effect in response to the terrorist attacks of September 11, 2001. In the following years, especially after the pro-immigrant marches of 2006 in several cities around the country, the church once again provided a safe haven to undocumented immigrants facing deportation orders, breathing new life into the sanctuary movement in churches in several states. The most publicized case was that of activist Elvira Arellano. Originally from Michoacan, Mexico, she had lived in a Methodist church in Chicago for a year and in 2007 decided to visit other sanctuary churches around the country to share her story. Arellano was arrested by immigration agents when she left La Placita, and was deported to Mexico.

Against this historical backdrop, La Placita has become the perfect stage for making important announcements on issues relating to immigration or the Mexican community. Visually, it possesses several attractive qualities that play very well in the media—the adobe buildings with tiled rooftops, the cobblestone streets, a huge mural of the Virgin of Guadalupe—under a banner made up of the flags of all the Latin American countries. Here, leaders of several churches announced an ecumenical alliance to support comprehensive immigration reform in 2006; and here activists held hunger strikes, demanding an end to deportations. The Mexican poet Javier Sicilia held his community-outreach events with members of the Caravan for Peace here, protesting the tragic consequences of the drug wars in Mexico resulting from US drug prohibition. Sicilia was photographed in La Placita with the biggest Mexican stars in Hollywood, playfully known as "Frijollywood": the directors Alejandro Gonzalez Iñarritu, Guillermo del Toro, and Alfonso Cuaron; the actors Diego Luna and Kate del Castillo; and the producers of *A Day Without a Mexican*, Yareli Arizmendi and Sergio Arau.

In early October 2012, another announcement was made at La Placita. The media were invited by Latinos for Obama, a volunteer group trying to strengthen voter participation among Latinos. They invited people to register to vote if they had not already done so and campaigned for Obama's reelection, explaining the benefits of Obama's platform for Latinos in contrast to that of his opponent, Mitt Romney. In their statement at the event, Latinos for Obama announced that the union leader Maria Elena Durazo, who had worked closely with Cesar Chavez's group and was highly respected by the community, would be there, along with Assemblyman Gil Cedillo, the DREAM Act's major supporter in California, and the keynote speaker, Senator Dick Durbin.

With his characteristically firm, unhurried gait, Durbin stepped onto the esplanade in front of La Placita, where reporters and cameras awaited. His impeccable navy-blue suit with gold buttons gave him a sober look, in contrast with his genial smile. His scarlet tie completed the look, perfect for the cameras. In his eleven years fighting for the DREAM Act, it was the first time that Senator

Durbin had visited Los Angeles for this kind of event. Obama's second term had to be in jeopardy, there had to be a real possibility of a Republican like Romney, explicitly opposed to the DREAM Act, taking control of the White House for Durbin to feel compelled to travel all the way to La Placita to talk about the importance of the Latino vote and the importance of a Deferred Action program being put into place, which would at least give the Dreamers a respite of two years, even if it did not provide any permanent solutions.

Durbin addressed a skeptical crowd that day. During his first presidential campaign, Obama had repeatedly expressed his support for the DREAM Act's passage and had said that one of the first things his administration would do would be to push comprehensive immigration reform through Congress. Not only did he accomplish neither of these two things in his first four years in office, his administration set a new record for deportations of undocumented immigrants: almost 1.5 million. Among the Latino community, Obama has earned the nickname "Deporter in Chief."

So at a time of crisis, the Democratic Party turned to its strongest sales team. But they still haven't been able to close the deal.

CHAPTER FOUR

———◆———

BACK TO A STRANGE WORLD

*Immigration policy should be generous; it should
be fair; it should be flexible. With such a policy
we can turn to the world, and to our own past,
with clean hands and a clear conscience.*

—JOHN F. KENNEDY, *A Nation of Immigrants*, 1958

ON A TUESDAY MORNING just like any other, Nancy Landa got
herself ready for work. Full-figured, with dark hair, olive skin, and
a bright smile, she put on black pants, a blouse, and low-heeled
pumps for her job at a government office in California. It was 2009,
and at twenty-nine, Nancy was the very picture of success. She had
graduated five years before with a degree in business administration from California State University, Northridge, and since then
she had doggedly climbed up the professional ladder, first in community service organizations and then in the public sector.

Nancy made sure she had everything she needed for the day in
her handbag: her wallet with forty dollars in it, credit and debit
cards just in case, and her ever-present cell phone. She left the
apartment she shared with her brother in Long Beach, in Los Angeles County, with plenty of time to get to the office. She got in her
car, which she had bought just a few months earlier and was still
paying off, and headed to the freeway.

While she was driving down Third Street, a white van ordered
her to pull over. It wasn't a Long Beach police or highway patrol
vehicle. But Nancy wasn't worried. She pulled over to the side of
the street, rolled her window down, and waited for the officer to

perhaps cite her for some minor infraction or alert her to something about her car that needed attention.

Then, her nightmare began. Three people stepped up to Nancy's car and informed her she was being detained. One of them,
a woman, announced they were immigration agents. "You know
why we're detaining you, right? Were you hiding from us?" said
another. They took her bag and escorted her into their vehicle, a
van with no identifying markings. Her car stayed right where it
was, parked haphazardly on the side of the road. Two hours later,
Nancy found herself in a detention center in downtown Los Angeles, and just eight hours later she was deported to Tijuana, Mexico,
with only the clothes on her back. She had no friends or family
there, no past. All she had was the handbag they had returned to
her once she was on the other side of the border, with the forty dollars, credit cards, and cell phone. And just like that, on an ordinary
Tuesday that had begun like any other, the life Nancy had built for
herself over the past twenty years was gone.

MORE PEOPLE CROSS through at the San Ysidro border station
than at any other in the world. Connecting Tijuana with San Diego, California, it processes more than thirty million people going
from Mexico into the United States every year, and it also processes
the most deportees going in the other direction. The deportees arrive by bus from detention centers, often from San Diego or Los
Angeles, and are put in a line in front of a turnstile with horizontal
metal bars. The revolving metal bars interlock with another set of
fixed metal bars, like teeth clamping down on a beast of prey. One
by one, the detainees shuffle into this metallic merry-go-round,
which rattles percussively as they take their one-way ride: *clack-
clack-clack-clack* there goes one, *clack-clack-clack-clack* there goes
another, *clack-clack-clack-clack* and another, and they emerge on
the other side in Mexico.

One of every five of the 1.8 million Mexicans whom immigration authorities have deported back to their country over the

past decade have returned through this metal turnstile. More than 350,000 people dumped in a place that most of them do not know at all, where there are no helpful indicators pointing the way to somewhere they can spend the night or get their next meal. Some are deported just a few days or even hours after having crossed the border, caught by *la migra* (immigration) as they tried to make their way to a big city where they could melt away into the crowd. These migrants may wind up passing through the metal turnstile, and they can more or less figure out what to do. But others, like Nancy, have spent virtually their entire lives in the United States, growing up and going to school, making friends, starting a career, and building a future there, until one day they are suddenly "returned" to a place that is completely foreign to them.

Nancy's family came to the United States when she was nine years old and her brother was seven. Nancy vaguely remembers living in subdivision 68 in Naucalpan, in the state of Mexico. They were very poor: her father would go off to California for long stretches to work and send money back home. When he would come back to Mexico to work, it was impossible to make ends meet, so one day he decided he wouldn't come back. Then Nancy's mother announced that they would all go together. It was April 1990.

"I remember myself then, as a girl, I was so angry with my mother. I remember telling her she was taking away everything I knew, because I would never see my friends again," Nancy tells me, taking a sip of coffee.

We got together one Sunday in Tijuana, where—deportation is destiny—she now lives. Dressed casually, seeming calm and relaxed, Nancy tells me about certain chapters in her life with a mix of nostalgia and resignation. It's been three years since she passed through the metal turnstile, and she has not been back to the United States. She feels comfortable here now, she says. She feels that people understand people like her, who speak Spanglish, don't have a past in Mexico, and have to remake their lives. Half of the people living in Tijuana are from somewhere else, and now Nancy is just one more.

"I thought it wasn't fair because I was doing well in school, I had been doing everything right up until then," she begins telling me as we sat out on the terrace of one of the most historical hotels in the city. The only time she had been in Tijuana before being deported was when her family had made the journey north across the border, twenty years earlier. "When we got here, my parents had already made all the arrangements with a coyote. I remember a room, maybe in a hotel, I'm not sure. When we got here it was very late at night, and from there they took us to cross over at three in the morning, when there would be no *migra*. My mom says we crossed running through Playas [a section of Tijuana]. Twenty years later, she pointed out the exact place where we crossed. Back then it was just a wasteland, now there's a big fence there, but I remember it was really hard for me to run, like when you're running on sand, so that makes sense. It took us all night to cross, and that's the only memory I have of Tijuana. My dad picked us up the next day, by then we were already in the United States."

From then on Nancy and her family lived in Los Angeles. Even though she and her brother didn't speak English when they arrived, they picked it up quickly and began attending school regularly and building a new life. Little Nancy blossomed into a young woman, graduated high school, and went on to college, where she was president of the student council and graduated with honors.

Her parents, meanwhile, were aware of the difficult circumstances their children would find themselves in when they enrolled in college or began looking for a job without documentation, so they sought out legal advice. They fell into the hands of a notary who worked in association with a lawyer. She assured them she could successfully make the case to legalize the family's status by arguing that returning to Mexico would put them in a situation of "extreme hardship," a term generally used in immigration cases when migrants seek asylum because returning to their countries of origin would put them in grave danger. As their case made its way through the system, a year after graduation Nancy received official permission to work and a Social Security number, which asylum seekers are entitled to by law while their cases are pending. With these documents in hand, Nancy could get a driver's license and apply for a job wherever she wanted. Her dream had come true.

Nancy worked in a district assemblyman's office in California. It was her job to promote scholarships and other resources for students, a mission that was deeply personal because of her own experience. "It was expensive for me because I was in school in 1998, before we were defined as Dreamers," she remembers. Her work evolved into trying to motivate students, telling them they could study even if they were undocumented, that they didn't have to give up. She told them that whether or not they stayed in the United States, their education would always be with them.

In 2008, Nancy received a notice from the notary: her case had been denied. From that moment on, her permission to work would not be renewed, and the family was once again undocumented. But that wasn't all. Once immigration authorities denied their case for asylum, the family's immigration status was on record. They could be deported at any time.

Around the same time, Nancy was accepted into HOPE (Hispanics Organized for Political Equality), an organization that awards grants providing leadership training to Latina women who play key roles in their communities. After eight months of training, Nancy traveled with the other members of her group to Washington, DC, for their graduation ceremony. Once there, she realized she would have to skip the ceremony, which was to be held in the Federal Reserve Building. A woman who was aware of her situation warned her that when she entered the building, they might ask her questions related to her status, so she decided not to go inside.

"The notary tricked us," Nancy said. "She knew, and I know now, that our case was not going to be decided in our favor. There was no way she could prove that our lives would be at risk if we went back to Mexico—asylum visas are only granted to Mexican citizens in exceptional cases. The most recent cases have been journalists who have been threatened by narco traffickers. I don't have anything to make my case: I'm not married to a US citizen, and I don't have a child who was born there. I had no basis for a case, and she knew it. The only thing she did was take my parents' money for seven years. The only hope I had was that the Dream Act would pass or if Obama had announced the Deferred Action program earlier, but no. Immigration came for me first."

NANCY WAS DETAINED ON SEPTEMBER 1. When the three immigration agents identified themselves, she did a double take. She looked at their faces and remembered that she had seen them just the day before: as she left her apartment building, they had been coming in. She had come face-to-face with them, but they didn't know who she was. They had been coming to take her into custody at her apartment, but they had missed her by just a few minutes. That's why one of them had accused her of hiding from them, she understood later.

"Why would they send three officials to arrest you?" she asks indignantly, showing a flash of anger for the first time. A waiter walking by our table hears her comment. He stops, wanting to listen in on our conversation. When he notices me looking at him he quickly walks away, somewhat embarrassed.

"I don't know how long they had been looking for me but it was at least two days, maybe more. I knew my work permit wasn't valid anymore and the lawyer had told me my case was closed, but I'm not a criminal. Three agents looking for me at all hours, like I'm some kind of dangerous criminal?"

Nancy had calmly gotten out of her car, thinking that somehow everything would be worked out. Or maybe she wasn't really thinking at all, and that's why her memory is so fuzzy. She remembers they patted her down but did not handcuff her. The agents were annoyed when she asked to call her family on her cell phone, and though it wasn't standard protocol, the female agent gave her permission. Nancy called her parents, but there was no answer. She left a message. She called a girlfriend, but she didn't pick up, either.

Nancy asked that her car not be left practically in the street, but they wouldn't let her go near it. They escorted her into the white van that drove around the streets of Los Angeles for what seemed like a very long time. Then suddenly they stopped in front of a school, the door opened, and a woman who looked to be about thirty years old got in. She was very upset, practically hysterical. Nancy tried to calm her down, and the woman explained she had just dropped her daughter off at kindergarten and she was the only person who could pick her up. She was a single mother, her daughter had special needs, and she didn't have anybody who could pick her up when school was over. Other than that, Nancy doesn't remember if they picked up more people in the van or not, and she doesn't remember how they got to the jail. She does remember that by eleven o'clock that morning, they were being processed in the Los Angeles detention center.

"Have you ever been there?" she asks me. For some reason I feel a little embarrassed when I admit I haven't. Then she tells me what it's like there.

Nancy was escorted into a large room inside the facility, with walls painted a cold, institutional white, where all the people who had been detained that day were held. Most of them were dressed for work. "They could have been my parents," Nancy says. Eight out of ten were men. Since she was dressed a little more formally than most, Nancy felt out of place. After they recorded her name and Social Security number and fingerprinted her, she was allowed to make a phone call. Like almost everyone who always uses a cell phone, Nancy did not know anybody's number from memory, so she asked if she could have her cell phone to look up the number. When they gave it back to her, Nancy started discreetly sending text messages to her family and contacts to let them know where she was. One of her coworkers in turn let other people know. Someone told her she could buy a phone card and use a pay phone in the detention center to make calls. She remembered the forty dollars she had quickly tucked into her pants pocket before they had taken her bag from her. She bought a twenty-dollar card. She made some calls, talked to the people she needed to talk to, and waited. The next few hours seemed endless.

Talking to some of the other women, she found out that the authorities had tried to pressure many of them into signing a consent form, affirming that they were leaving the country voluntarily. By signing the form, a detainee officially accepts that he or she is undocumented, and the deportation process begins. Many people who refuse to sign and have some sort of previous violation on record, such as a DUI, are held in detention centers for months until an immigration judge is assigned to hear their case. As time goes by in detention, their growing desperation becomes their enemy and the authorities' ally. Wanting to get out of there as soon as possible after languishing in detention, they end up signing the consent form and accepting their deportation, even though for most, just getting their cases on a judge's docket can help gain them a few more years in the country, since it can take that long for the cases to be heard in the backlogged immigration court system.

"It was clear to me that many of the people there did not have legal counsel," Nancy says. "And things get very complicated even for the people who do have lawyers. They insist that you sign something. I said I would not sign anything until my lawyer got there. I asked if I was going to go before a judge, and nobody answered me. A friend from work came to see me, and the people from HOPE had asked the Mexican consulate in Los Angeles to send a representative. But they couldn't do anything. An official from immigration came into the room where I was talking to the man from the consulate, and she said the next bus to Tijuana was ready. She told the man from the consulate that I had an order of deportation already so I would not be going before a judge. Of course, I never saw that deportation order."

The buses that transport deportees to Tijuana are white, impersonal. They are filled mostly with men, but there is a small section reserved for women in the front. That's where Nancy sat for the almost four-hour drive down Freeway 5, at rush hour's peak: through East Los Angeles, past Disneyland, the San Onofre nuclear plant, past the Marine base at Camp Pendleton and the beautiful beaches of San Diego. She did not think about how these were her last hours in the United States or that she would soon be leaving behind everything she knew. Nancy was just worried about what she would do when she got to Mexico. Whom should she get in touch with? It was getting dark. Where would she spend the night?

Once they arrived at San Ysidro, just moments before crossing the border into Mexico, Nancy was given a document with her "alien" number on it, registering her as a deported foreigner, and a paper bag containing her handbag. She was relieved to discover her cell phone still had a signal, so she began sending text messages. She went through the metal revolving gate, *clack-clack-clack*, and stepped out of the world she knew. Welcome to Mexico.

Once over the border in Mexican territory, security is handled by Grupo Beta, an agency that protects migrants and operates under the auspices of the National Institute of Migration of the Secretary of the Interior. Grupo Beta was created in Tijuana in 1990, and now there are twenty-one branches operating in nine Mexican states, located directly along the country's northern and southern borders or in states where migrants tend to pass through. The objective of the agency, according to its statutes, is to "save the lives of migrants in danger in high-risk areas." Nancy found out that the assistance offered by Grupo Beta came in two forms: offering to pay half of the price of a bus ticket back to migrants' home towns, if that's where they wanted to go, or helping them make a phone call through a computer. Neither of these options was of any use to Nancy.

"My head was spinning. How safe is Tijuana? How will it be for me here as a single woman? How can I protect myself? It was clear to me that I was entering a completely unknown world. Even though it's your country, it doesn't feel like your country. Even now, three years later, people tell me I don't sound Mexican when I talk. Three years ago it was much worse. So the first thing I thought was I should not talk too much, to not attract attention, and I would have to ask somebody to tell me where I could find a safe place to spend the night."

That "somebody" turned out to be three of her girlfriends, who sent her a message saying they were on their way to Tijuana to help her. They arrived four hours later, at around midnight. As soon as she saw them, Nancy started sobbing. Another friend who had stayed behind managed to find a place Nancy could stay for two days, with a girl she knew who lived there. Then, the girl talked to her grandfather and worked it out so that Nancy could stay with him for a longer period. Fully aware of how lucky she was to have gotten this help, Nancy wondered how it was for other people in her situation who were not as fortunate. Still, her new temporary residence was hardly an ideal place to stay for any length of time. The family hosting her was of very humble means, and their neighborhood reminded Nancy of her early childhood in Mexico City's subdivision 68. The buildings were covered in graffiti; there were lots of men hanging around the streets, and Nancy saw no one who looked like herself. And as she landed in this strange place, Nancy had her first encounters with Mexico's baffling bureaucracy.

Shopping. Nancy had arrived with the clothes she wore. As it turned out, the girl she stayed with that first night sold clothing. Nancy still had the twenty dollars left from the detention center and her credit cards. She went to an ATM to withdraw some cash. Luckily, she had enough money saved up to live on for a few weeks, if she budgeted carefully. There she discovered that she could withdraw only five thousand pesos. She had no idea how much this was in dollars or what she could buy with this amount. How much did things cost in Mexico? A pair of pants could cost thirty pesos, or three hundred, or maybe three thousand?

The phone. Her cell phone still had a signal, but she couldn't afford to incur roaming charges, especially since she didn't even know how to pay for them. She decided to buy a Mexican cell phone. The clerk asked her for identification. She showed him her consular matriculate.

"What's this?" the sales clerk asked.

"It's the consular matriculate, my identification."

"We don't accept this. Don't you have your IFE card?"

"What's that?" Nancy asked.

When they finally agreed to accept the matriculate as identification, they asked her for an RFC, or taxpayer identification number, in order to activate the phone. Of course, Nancy had never heard of this number, with the initials that reminded her of the fried chicken chain KFC. The wife of the girl's grandfather who she was staying with gave Nancy her number to use. When it was time to pay, Nancy tried to use her credit card. Once again they asked for identification. She presented her matriculate. They would not accept it. In the same store where they had accepted the matriculate as identification to sell her a phone, they would not accept it to prove that she was the actual owner of the credit card. Nancy went to an ATM to withdraw the 1,500 pesos to buy the phone.

The following weekend, a friend visited from Los Angeles to bring her some of her things: personal documents, her laptop, and some clothes. Her friend was shocked to see the conditions she was living in. "Nancy, you have to get out of here," was all he could manage to say. They spent two days searching for an apartment in an area nearby, and they found one that was available. Nancy did the math: if she tapped into her savings, she could pay five months' rent, spending the bare minimum on everything else. She hoped that within that time she could find a job. Now, all she needed was to sign the lease and pay the first month's rent.

The IFE. It was clear to Nancy that if she wanted to have access to basic services, she had to apply for an IFE card from the Federal Electoral Institute. The card had been designed to be used as identification when going to the polls, but over time it has become an all-purpose ID for official transactions in Mexico. She was told to show up early to fill out an application, so she got to the office at six o'clock in the morning. But it was already too late, because they would accept only a limited quota of applications per day. The next time Nancy arrived at four in the morning and was able to submit her application. Her IFE card arrived in the mail several weeks later, after she had already managed to use other forms of identification to successfully rent and move into her own apartment.

Money. Nancy had six thousand dollars in the bank. With-drawing small amounts of cash from ATMs turned out to be some-what complicated, since her bank in the United States might flag all the withdrawals in Mexico as suspicious activity and freeze her account. So she decided to make use of the wonders of technol-ogy, making transfers to some of her friends' bank accounts over the Internet and having them bring the cash to her the next time they were able to visit. Seven people came to visit over the next few weeks. A group of former coworkers from her first job took up a collection for Nancy and presented her with $1,500. As she tells me this, Nancy breaks down in tears for the first time in our conversation. She describes that scene for me, her voice breaking: "I didn't know what to say to them, because I've never asked for money from anybody. I've always been very independent. But I realized that I couldn't say no, it was exactly what I needed at the time. That was all I had to get by. I was so grateful, I don't know if I'll ever be able to pay them back someday."

Her network of friends in the United States, the money she had in the bank, knowing how to make good use of communication technology, and access to the Internet: Nancy understands exactly what tools and support she relied on to help her begin a new life in Tijuana. But not a day goes by that she doesn't wonder how other people manage who arrive in Tijuana like she did with just the clothes they are wearing but without any of the support she had. It was all she could talk about that first weekend when her friend came to visit, as they took a ride in his car along the border.

"It's interesting to me. Since I've been here I've taken pictures and videos of it. We're literally just a step away from the United States. I can touch the border and there it is, the physical bor-der and the immigration laws we have in place that divide us—the system sees everything in black and white. It doesn't look at peo-ple's individual circumstances. For me, that process was inhumane. They treated me like a common criminal. At one point my friend got out of the car and showed me the federal police carrying their big guns, so I wouldn't get scared when I saw them walking around the city. Then we went to Playas de Tijuana and I found a Star-bucks!" She laughs. "Finally, something familiar!"

ON OCTOBER 1, 2009, exactly one month after Nancy was deported, a friend called her.

"I wanted to let you know so you're prepared: they detained your mom and dad and your brother; they're going to send them to Tijuana."

For a fraction of a second, her mind went blank. She didn't feel panicked, or angry, or even surprised. A vast emptiness washed over her for just an instant and then lifted. When Nancy got in touch with her family, very calmly she described what it would be like when they got there, and she told them where they would find a McDonald's very near the border station. She asked them to wait for her there and said that she would come to pick them up. At least she had a place for them to stay, and they would all be together again.

The family decided to stay in Tijuana. During her first three years there, Nancy managed to move into a more comfortable apartment by herself, and she found a job working for a major United States company that manufactures electronics in Tijuana. She started in their telephone center and has moved up to their design department. She has made an effort to adapt to her new reality and acknowledges that the education she received in the United States and her bilingualism have opened doors for her. Still, her inability to return to what she considers her country has limited her professional development: when her presence is required at high-level meetings at corporate headquarters, Nancy is unable to attend.

On June 15, 2012, Nancy found out through the news and from her friends that President Obama had announced the Deferred Action program, which would benefit undocumented students who had entered the United States as minors. But it came three years too late for the Landa family.

———◆———

June 17, 2012
The Honorable Barack Obama, President of the United States
The White House
1600 Pennsylvania Avenue NW
Washington, DC 20500
RE: Order to End Deportation of Young Undocumented Immigrants

Dear Mr. President:

I was moved to know that after 26 years of inertia, there is now in place a policy that will allow young undocumented immigrants to integrate themselves into the fabric of American society. At the same time, it was hard for me to accept that this reform came almost three years too late for my brother and I, whom would have otherwise qualified. Instead, we were deported at age 27 and 29, respectively.

Starting at the age of nine, I was part of a class of people that lived in the shadows afraid to be exposed due to our legal status. Despite these challenges, I excelled academically and graduated in the top three percent of my high school class. I went on to earn my B.S. degree. I was an active participant in my community offering countless volunteer hours to further social causes.

Four years ago I thought your candidacy offered the hope we needed to change the direction of the country including its current immigration laws. Although I could not vote for you, I volunteered on your campaign believing that reform could be possible. The reality is that under your administration, deportation of non-criminal undocumented immigrants has increased and has contributed to more family separations than during the eight years of the George W. Bush presidency. The failure to take action earlier has irreversibly impacted the lives of hundreds of immigrants that are thrown out of the United States on a daily basis. I and my family are among that number.

I was forced out of a country I called home without the opportunity to collect my financial documents or a change of clothes that would have allowed me to sustain myself that first week in Tijuana. Yet I continue to live with limited professional prospects in my native country due to current US policies.

I write to you now, to request three changes that would make a difference for people like me:

1. Increasing accountability of the Customs Enforcement Agency and their deportation procedures
2. Removing the 10-year ban for deportees so they can successfully appeal their cases
3. Reforming the visa process so deportees who are working in their country of origin and are required to travel to the US for business purposes are not ineligible for a visitor's visa

What I really hope for is true immigration reform that provides the 12 million undocumented immigrants a pathway to citizenship. In the meantime, implementing the above changes will make the current legal process more humane.

Most respectfully,
Nancy Landa
Tijuana, Baja California, Mexico

In response, she received this letter from the president.

Dear Nancy:

Thank you for writing. I have heard from many Americans concerned about immigration and I appreciate your perspective.

Americans are rightly frustrated with our Nation's broken immigration system, and I share that frustration. We need an immigration system that meets America's 21st-century economic and security needs. We can achieve such a system only by putting aside politics and coming together to develop a comprehensive solution that continues to secure our borders, holds businesses responsible for who they hire, strengthens our economic competitiveness, and requires undocumented immigrants to get right with the law. That is how we can reaffirm our heritage as a Nation of immigrants and a Nation of laws.

My Administration has invested an unprecedented amount of resources, technology, and manpower to secure our borders, and our efforts are producing real results. Today, our Southern border is more secure than ever, with more law enforcement personnel than at any time in American history—and there are fewer illegal crossings now than at any time in the past 40 years. Crime rates along the border are down, and we have seized more illegal guns, cash, and drugs than in years past. In addition to doing what is necessary to secure our borders, my Administration is implementing a smart, effective immigration enforcement policy which includes taking action against employers who knowingly exploit people and break the law, as well as against criminal immigrants who pose a threat to safety of American communities.

Stopping illegal immigration also depends upon reforming our outdated system of legal immigration. My Administration is working to strengthen and streamline the legal immigration system through administrative reforms, making it easier for employers, immigrants, and families to navigate the system. For example, we have reduced barriers to citizenship by keeping application fees constant and providing and creating tools to help applicants through the naturalization process. Through the innovative "Entrepreneurs in Residence" initiative, we are streamlining existing pathways for foreign-born entrepreneurs to come and create businesses and jobs in our country. Finally, we are working to support families by addressing a serious barrier in the law which requires Americans to risk years of separation from their loved ones, particularly spouses and children, in order to process a family visa petition. By proposing a waiver before these families separate, we are advancing legal immigration and the reunification of families—both fundamental principles under the law.

I remain deeply committed to working in a bipartisan way to enact immigration reform that restores accountability and responsibility to our broken immigration system. The Federal Government has the responsibility to continue to secure our borders. Those immigrants who are here illegally have a responsibility to pay taxes, pay a fine, learn English, and undergo background checks before they can get on a path to earn legal status. At the same time, we need to provide businesses a legal way to hire the workers they rely on, and a path for those workers to earn legal status.

The law should also stop punishing young people who were brought to this country as children by giving them a chance to stay and earn a legal status if they pursue higher education or serve in our military. In the absence of any action on immigration from Congress, my Administration will continue to focus our enforcement resources on high-priority individuals, including those who present national security or public safety concerns and those who have recently entered our country. As another step in this process, on June 15, 2012, the Department of Homeland Security announced it will allow eligible young people who do not present a risk to our national security or public safety to request temporary relief from deportation proceedings and apply for work authorization. This is not a path to citizenship, and it is not a permanent fix—only Congress can provide that. This is only a temporary measure to allow us to focus our resources wisely while giving a degree of relief and hope to talented, driven, and patriotic young people.

By creating a 21st-century immigration system that is true to our principles, our Nation will remain a land of opportunity, prosperity, and freedom for all. To learn more about my Administration's efforts regarding immigration, or to read our Blueprint for Immigration Reform, please visit *www.WhiteHouse.gov/Issues/Immigration.* For additional information and resources on current immigration and enforcement efforts, I encourage you to visit *www.DHS.gov* or call 1-800-375-5283.

Thank you, again, for writing.

Sincerely,
Barack Obama

How can 140 countries live together in one place? That's the challenge the city of Los Angeles has had to face so that a group of people speaking 224 distinct languages can harmoniously coexist in the same community. And they have met the challenge well. Residents and visitors to the City of Angels can easily go from downtown to Chinatown, or Filipinotown, or Koreatown, or Little

Armenia, Little Ethiopia, Little Tokyo, or Thai Town, to name just a few, and sit at restaurants and enjoy the cuisines each of these communities have brought with them from their countries. Enjoying a fresh Oacaxan mole, pad thai with artisanal noodles, or going out with friends for authentic Korean barbecue are everyday pleasures for Los Angelenos. When you have lived in a world this culturally diverse, it can be very hard to leave it behind.

"There was a Vietnamese restaurant in Silver Lake, that was my favorite," Nancy tells me, nostalgic, when I ask her what she misses about the United States. "I miss that food; you can't find it here. There is Chinese food all over the place, but if I'm in the mood for Greek, Cuban, or Korean food, that's not easy to find in Tijuana. But I have had the best Mexican food of my whole life here."

The wave of nostalgia disappears when we start talking about the letter she sent to President Obama and his response. Her expression hardens, portraying a mix of disbelief and controlled rage.

"I'm still really angry," she says. "It's my country, but they threw me out; that still hurts a lot. It hurts knowing that the Deferred Action program came too late for me and knowing that, even after announcing it, they keep on deporting young people that do meet the program's requirements. That's why I decided to write to him, to tell him about my experience. I didn't do it for myself; I did it for the people around me, for all the stories I hear every day. I'm happy for everybody that will benefit from the program, but what about the ex-Dreamers? How are we doing outside of the country? Does anybody remember us, or think about the obstacles we have to overcome just to survive, or how we're going to manage?

"So I sent off that letter, and two months later I got that reply. A typical politician's response: a form letter. In one part at the end he says they are focusing on high-priority cases that pose a threat to national security, and deportations are based on that. So I'm a high-priority criminal and that's why I got deported?! He sends that to me as a response? He sends a form letter? They didn't even read my letter. They just sent me this reply they had all prepared. The really ironic thing is they send it to *me*, somebody who has actually been deported. That says a lot about his administration."

The time comes to say good-bye, and Nancy stands up. She seems taller, confident, in control. She has a charisma about her. As we walk out, she seems to radiate a special strength, reflecting her ability to get the most out of even the smallest resources she has to draw from. But she also looks tired. Once more, our conversation turns to Tijuana.

"I have come to love this city, because it's not what I thought it would be," she says. "I think my life is less stressful now. It has to do with the different pace things move at here compared with the United States, and my priorities have changed. Before, my career was what mattered most to me, to keep on moving up. Then you get to this point where you lose everything, you have to start over from the very beginning, and you decide you just want to enjoy life and not necessarily land some super amazing job. I know I have to keep fighting, especially since I see there is potential here in Mexico, so I don't see why we shouldn't have the quality of life that we deserve."

"The other problem is sexism," she says. "Where I am now, 80 percent of the professionals are men, and I don't get the same credit as they do, even though I do the same job. I know I'm paid less than other people with the same job, and I work harder. There are things that make me really mad about Mexico, in terms of equality, labor laws, discrimination. . . . But one fight at a time."

CHAPTER FIVE

◆

CALIFORNIA DREAMING

We absolutely know that education is for life.
Legal status is temporary.

—GIL CEDILLO, California state assemblyman

FOR GIL CEDILLO, April 5, 2012, was a glorious night. The Coalition for Humane Immigrant Rights in Los Angeles (CHIRLA) was holding its annual gala in the Park Plaza Hotel, a beautiful neo-Gothic building next to the Mexican consulate and across from MacArthur Park, in the heart of the city's Central American community. Gil, a state assemblyman, was the featured honoree.

The evening opened as these kinds of events usually do, with state and local officials chatting with leaders of civic organizations, academics talking with their peers, and activists exchanging business cards and making contacts. Some artists were there, donating original works to be auctioned, with the proceeds benefiting the organization hosting the event, since fund-raising is the main purpose of these generally rather boring affairs. Others buy tickets and attend just because they want to be a part of the scene. Over the course of the evening, they will all talk to a journalist at some point.

There was one unusual element that caught my attention as I climbed the grand, red-carpeted staircase under an impressive chandelier, leading up to a landing with marble columns supporting three archways: young college students, some of whom looked familiar, were there, all dressed up for the occasion. They talked with one another and mingled with politicians and professors. They were Dreamers, students from several universities, looking very polished in their finest clothes, smiling brightly, so excited to be a part of the night honoring Gil.

"He's coming," a girl said to her companion when Gil walked toward them.

They both stood tall, flashing broad smiles as the guest of honor offered them a warm handshake and a pat on the shoulder.

Gil may be the most well regarded Chicano politician in Southern California and perhaps in the entire United States. The son of a steel worker and a seamstress, he grew up in Boyle Heights, a neighborhood in East LA known for welcoming immigrants throughout the past century. The first newcomers were Jewish, who were later joined by Japanese Americans and then by immigrants from Mexico. Now, nine in ten residents in Boyle Heights are Latino, and almost half of those were born in Mexico.

In the late sixties, Gil attended Roosevelt High, where he met his friend Antonio Villaraigosa, who would go on to become mayor of Los Angeles. Gil majored in sociology at UCLA and later studied law at the Peoples College of Law, a school with a progressive philosophy that would have an influence on his political career, although he never did pass the bar exam. Of medium height, Gil carries himself with confidence and has a dark complexion, dark hair, ever-present circles under his eyes, and a pronounced cleft chin. Over the course of his career as a politician, Gil has come to be identified with two issues: the fight to allow undocumented immigrants to obtain driver's licenses and his efforts to pass a state-level DREAM Act in California.

A YEAR BEFORE THIS SPECIAL NIGHT, Gil Cedillo had addressed his colleagues in the state legislature in an attempt to convince them of the necessity of passing his proposal. Modeled after the federal DREAM Act, Gil's legislative package included similar age and length-of-residency requirements, and it would allow its beneficiaries to continue their studies and be eligible to receive private and public financial aid offered by the state, just like documented students in the state—though undocumented students would still be ineligible for federal aid. Since the California DREAM Act would become a state law, it would not change the students' immigration status, but it would give them access to a higher education that otherwise would be out of reach financially to many of them.

This was not the first time Gil had presented the initiative. In 2006, when he was a state senator, Gil had presented the first version of the law, SB 160, which passed in both houses of the state legislature only to be vetoed by the governor, Arnold Schwarzenegger. A year later, Gil presented it again, this time under the name SB 65, but it did not make it out of committee. In 2007, it was put on the table for the third time, with some changes meant to avoid a veto from the governor. Even with those adjustments, and despite the bill once more passing in both houses of the state legislature, Schwarzenegger vetoed it again.

Although Gil insisted on bringing up the initiative for a fourth time, it was clear to him and to other supporters of the California DREAM Act that they would have the best chance for success if they waited until after the November 2010 elections. With Schwarzenegger nearing the end of his second term in office and ineligible for a third term, Republican business executive Meg Whitman would face the veteran Democrat Jerry Brown in the race for governor.

In her fifties, blonde, full-figured with a bright, dimpled smile, Whitman was a brilliantly successful executive, originally from Long Island, New York. A graduate of Princeton University and the Harvard School of Business, she had worked in key positions for the Walt Disney Company, DreamWorks, Procter & Gamble, and Hasbro. Her crowning professional achievement came when she took over as president and CEO of the online auction site eBay, which over ten years grew from thirty employees to more than fifteen thousand and saw its earnings jump from $4 million to $8 billion annually. At the time of the gubernatorial election, Whitman was the fourth-richest woman in California, with a fortune of $13 billion, according to *Forbes*.

For his part, Jerry Brown came from a storied political family. The son of Pat Brown, California's thirty-second governor,

Jerry Brown had served as governor of the state from 1975 until 1983. He had gone on to serve as Democratic state chair, mayor of Oakland, and state attorney general, a position he occupied during Governor Schwarzenegger's second term. With decades of experience in politics, Brown, now in his seventies, came across as self-assured and determined, with a wiry frame and sharply receding hairline, his jaw set.

A win for Whitman would mean a continuation of Schwarzenegger's policies and maybe even a harder line on immigration issues, since right-wing Republicans strongly supported her. A victory for Brown would open the door to finally passing the California DREAM Act. During her campaign, Whitman made some ultimately unsuccessful overtures to the Latino community. She opened up a campaign office in East Los Angeles, where she was more often booed than cheered, and spent her own money on an unprecedented scale, pouring $144 million into her campaign, the most any candidate had spent in an electoral campaign in the country's history—on top of the $178 million her supporters had donated. In spite of Whitman's deep pockets, Brown carried the day on November 2, receiving 53 percent of the vote, while 40 percent went to Whitman.

With Brown back in the governor's office, beginning his term on January 3, 2011, State Assemblyman Gil Cedillo introduced his proposal yet again, this time dividing it into two initiatives, known as AB 130 and AB 131. The first established that students would have access to private funds—meaning scholarships from foundations, corporations, or private individuals—to help pay for their education. The second specified that students would also be eligible to receive financial aid provided by the state. This time, opponents added a new argument to their arsenal, usually grounded in immigration themes: the serious budget deficit that California had to contend with meant that the governor would have to make cuts in higher-education budgets. According to the measure's vocal critics, passing these laws would mean financially punishing students who were in the country legally, by giving "special treatment" to undocumented students.

On May 5, 2011, the first of the two initiatives came up for a vote. Moments before, Gil addressed his colleagues in the legislature:

> There is a body of law that makes it very clear, and convincing, that undocumented immigrants in fact do have rights. It's a lie that they don't. If you look to the very foundation of our constitution, the 14th Amendment says very clearly that no person shall be abridged of their rights to be treated fairly and equally. And every economist I talk to says that by 2025 we are going to be missing one million people from our economy who have BA and BS degrees, bachelor of arts and bachelor of science degrees we're going to be missing because of the demographic changes that are taking place.

Groups of students sat in the galleries of the state legislature in Sacramento, watching the session unfold below. Wearing black T-shirts emblazoned with slogans supporting the legislation, they hung on every word. A girl dressed in a cap and gown served as a visual reminder of what they were fighting for.

Sitting next to Gil, the Republican Assembly member Tim Donnelly waited for his turn to argue against the measure. The third child of fourteen, originally from Atlanta, he had gone to college in California and had been a small-business owner until he got involved in the Minuteman Project, a group often derided as vigilantes trying to secure the border with Mexico and deter undocumented migrants on their own. In his forties, almost bald, sporting a goatee and wearing glasses, Donnelly comes across as friendly and affable, qualities that surely helped him when he decided to found the Minuteman Party in California. In 2010 he appealed to the ultraconservative Tea Party vote to win the Republican nomination and then a seat in the State Assembly.

> I rise today in opposition to this bill, but I do so with a heavy heart. I appreciate the sentiments of my seatmate. I understand the unintended consequences of what is going on where you have

people who are brought here through no will of their own. We are not here to debate how we feel about things. We're not here to debate whether or not . . . somebody should help these students. And I say to you that this law will undermine the rule of law. It puts legal immigrants who are waiting in a long line, perhaps even from the same country, at a disadvantage.

Then a third speaker addressed the room: Democrat Mike Davis, an African American politician with a stocky build and the clear, even voice of a natural orator. Originally from North Carolina and a Harvard graduate, Davis represented District 48 in Los Angeles. At the end of his remarks, he addressed the students directly.

This is an important issue, because students who have done everything that they are supposed to do, who have completed what they have started academically, deserve to have an opportunity for higher education in this country. It is, in fact, the American Dream. The dream is an American Dream, and just a few years ago, we never anticipated that a little black boy from Illinois could overcome a Herculean challenge to become for the first time that the earth has ever known the president of the free world. His name is Barack Obama. And the same dream that he has achieved, you can, and you will, as well.

The first part of the proposed legislation was passed that day with fifty-one votes in favor and twenty-one against. A few days later it received the majority of votes in the Senate, and later, the second part of the legislation was also passed by a vote of forty-five to twenty-seven. Jerry Brown signed AB 130 into law on June 25, 2011, and AB 131 later that same year, on October 8.

A VIDEO SHOWN at the gala at the Park Plaza culminated with footage from the final vote on the Assembly floor. The students who had produced the short film included parts of Gil's speech made just before the vote and a montage of images from the DREAM Act's earliest beginnings up to the moment it was signed into law. The after-dinner conversations rising from the tables throughout the ballroom suddenly stopped when the images came onto the screen: Gil walking with some students; Gil in a meeting with them; students taking part in protests and marches; the speech given right before the vote; the electronic vote tally in the Assembly, with a cut to Gil anxiously turning to look at the count. When the voice of the president of the Assembly was heard announcing the results of the vote, everyone in the ballroom at the Gala burst into applause. The Dreamers and everyone else whooped and cheered, as if the vote had just happened.

Then Gil was introduced. Everyone rose to their feet and clapped as he came out onto the dais, smiling broadly, and the audience took their seats again. Then, from tables all across the room, in the front and in the back, one by one, students stood and made their way to the dais. We all watched in wonder as these finely dressed young people approached Gil. These were model students, who had been recognized by their schools for their achievements; students who had to fight every day just to stay in school because they had to work too; the ones who do everything that is asked of them and more, who lack only a little piece of paper that would somehow legitimize them. That night they enveloped Gil, hugged him, and shared their heartfelt emotion with him.

"It was wonderful. It was like an exploding star," Gil recalled.

This was his night, and Gil's smile could not have been any brighter.

A FEW WEEKS AFTER THE GALA, I met with Gil Cedillo in Los Angeles. Gil represents District 45, in the city's northeast. His office is there, in a fairly new office-and-residential complex in Highland Park, a Latino neighborhood. A young man and woman greeted me with smiles and told me to go up a flight of stairs to reach Gil's office. On the next floor I saw a door on either side of a small vestibule, and I chose to try the one on the right. I stepped through the door, and two young assistants sitting at their desks offered me polite smiles but didn't say anything. I almost felt bad for distracting them from what seemed to be a great deal of pending tasks that demanded their full concentration. Just as I was considering whether I should go back into the hall and try the other door, I saw Gil with a few other people in a far corner of the room.

At fifty-eight, Gil shows his age in the lines on his face, which are more noticeable now after he followed his doctor's orders and shed some pounds, going on a strict diet and running three to five miles every morning. He has big, expressive eyes that could look very happy when he smiles, if it weren't for the dark circles underneath that have become a sort of trademark. The day I met with him he seemed tired, and the circles looked even darker than usual, but at the same time he looked very relaxed and smiled warmly. He was wearing dress pants and a blue shirt, and he greeted me with a kiss on the cheek. He was waiting for the arrival of the documentary filmmaker Hector Cruz Sandoval, who was working on a film about the California DREAM Act and would be coming that day to get some footage. Gil invited me into his office, the room on the left. When we went in he stretched, trying to shake off the fatigue.

I was surprised by how much bright light streamed into his office, a cozy, comfortable space that still felt like it belonged to a politician. His desk was in a corner, while a comfortable sitting area occupied the middle of the room. Before even asking me to sit down, Gil started showing me some of the artwork hanging on the walls. First he pointed out a pair of paintings, portraits of him and the woman he calls "the love of my life," his wife, Ruby, who died of cancer in 2002. The artist was George Gonzalez, and Gil emphasized the date the portraits were made: 2001. "Before Obama," he said, with a satisfied grin. The painting does look very much like the emblematic portrait that Los Angeles artist Shepard Fairey did for Barack Obama's presidential campaign in 2008, in reds and blues with the word "Hope," that became a fixture on social media that year. An app even came out that let users "Obamicize" their own picture, inserting the word of their choice. But the portraits of Gil were in that style seven years earlier, he tells me.

Aside from the Gonzalez painting, there were some other interesting pieces in the office. On a bookcase was one of the variations the artist Luis Genaro Garcia produced of the iconic traffic sign, in this case depicting three black figures over a bright yellow backdrop, representing a fleeing migrant family. The sign is used on highways near the border to alert drivers to exercise caution in areas where undocumented migrants may be attempting to cross. The image usually shows the figure of a man running, pulling along a woman behind him, and she in turn grasps the hand of a small child behind her. Garcia's version shows three people in the same stance but dressed in graduation caps and gowns, clutching diploma scrolls in their hands. The image is very popular among Dreamers. At the CHIRLA gala a few months earlier, some versions of this work signed by the author were among the best-selling items during the fund-raising auction.

Of course, like any Chicano leader, Gil had to have a Virgin of Guadalupe nearby; the one in his office, made of brass, was very eye-catching. A large window was in between the sitting area and his desk, a large wood table off to the side with two chairs for guests. A black-and-white work by an artist named Rodriguez took up most of the wall over the desk. It depicts a scene under a bridge in Boyle Heights, the neighborhood where Gil grew up. Gesturing toward the picture, he began telling me the story that he probably tells everybody whom he sees looking at it: "We first lived on Eighth Street, and then we moved to Fourth Street. That's where I spent my childhood, and I used to go and sit under this bridge." He said this so solemnly that I couldn't help but imagine Gil as a young boy, sitting right there under that bridge in Los Angeles in the 1960s.

Gil Cedillo was born in 1954 in Barstow, a town in the California desert located exactly halfway between Los Angeles and Las Vegas. The town is known for being close to a Marine base in the Mojave Desert and for having been used as a backdrop in popular movies such as *Gattaca* and *Kill Bill: Vol. 2*. A few years later the family moved to Los Angeles, which meant Gil would grow up during the height of the Chicano rights movement.

Although the word "Chicano" is used colloquially to refer to Mexican Americans, it means more than that. Not everyone with a Mexican background was part of the Chicano movement, and some who were had roots in other countries, like Guatemala or El Salvador. Identifying as Chicano has more to do with a cultural and political identity than mere geography.

The movement began in the 1960s and was active on several fronts. One was the fight for farmworker rights headed by Cesar Chavez, leader of the first large-scale movement to organize Latino workers in the United States, which would become the United Farm Workers (UFW). Chavez organized several worker strikes and a national boycott of grapes, an effort that gained the movement supporters and sympathizers from all backgrounds across the country and succeeded in reforming the grape industry. But that's not all Chavez accomplished: he also sparked a civil rights movement among the Mexican American community, just as the country reeled from the assassinations of Martin Luther King Jr. and Robert F. Kennedy and as protests of the Vietnam War heated up. By the end of the decade, the movement grappled with a range of issues, including pushing for the right to vote and political access, fighting ethnic stereotypes, and ensuring equal access to education.

Another branch of activism in the Mexican American community was spearheaded by Humberto "Bert" Corona, who also founded the Center for Autonomous Social Action (CASA) in 1969 in an effort to establish a framework for Mexican immigrant workers to connect and help one another and to provide other social services. Corona's ideology was a blend of Mexican nationalism—he was the son of a colonel in Pancho Villa's army and had lived through the Mexican revolution and revolutionary upheaval along the border in Ciudad Juarez and El Paso—Marxist-Leninist philosophy, and the intellectual ideals of the brothers Ricardo and Enrique Flores Magon, who were also in Los Angeles at the time. CASA decided to reject the "Chicano" label and sought to erase the differences between Mexicans from Mexico and Mexican Americans, asserting that those kinds of categorizations serve capitalism and its need to preserve a subservient class of workers.

The ideal of Mexicans without borders was the guiding principle of the movement.

Within this context, youth movements inspired by the African American civil rights struggle developed, some with a student element, including United Mexican American Students (UMAS) and later the Chicano Student Movement of Aztlan, or Movimiento Estudiantil Chicano de Aztlan (MEChA), aiming to open up access to power for Chicano youth. Another notable group was the Brown Berets, whose issues included promoting the right to high-quality nutrition, housing, and employment.

In March 1968, more than a thousand students at Abraham Lincoln High School in East Los Angeles, the heart of the Chicano movement, staged a walkout to protest their school's deplorable conditions. The peaceful protest, supported by a teacher, Sal Castro, was copied in other Los Angeles schools, and more than ten thousand students walked out of classes over the course of just a few days. To this day, the East Los Angeles walkouts are the largest high school student protests to have taken place in the country.

Gil Cedillo was a student at Roosevelt High, one of the participating schools. His eyes shine brightly with pride when he talks about those years and his participation in the protest movement and his friendship with Villaraigosa; he swells with pride in the same way when he talks about the young people who worked so hard alongside him to get the California DREAM Act passed. The spark is the same with the Dreamers, he asserts—I see it in his eyes when he's halfway through his story—because they can view their own participation in an optimistic way.

"It started for me when I was fifteen, but really it was even earlier," says Gil. "Movements like this, like Bert Corona's, like MEChA, are one part of a bigger story." He goes on to tell me about similar movements started by groups of different students and movements in other countries, making circular motions with his hands as he talks, describing a continuum that, as outlined by a tenacious politician who never gives up, sounds almost idyllic. Mexican Americans contribute to the struggle waged by African Americans; students talk about morals and ethics, educational reform and Vietnam; students fight for the rights of immigrants as members of the larger community. It's a never-ending struggle, Gil says, one that transfers easily, like college credit for a history class, to his position as an assemblyman as he denounces budget cuts that put universities and the quality of higher education in jeopardy.

"So in a way, we're still fighting for those spaces for immigrant students, to make sure there is enough room for everybody. That's where we're heading," he sums up, satisfied that he conveyed the idea of his generation passing along the torch to the Dreamers.

But the road has not always been smooth. One moment of discord that had a profound impact on Gil took place while he was in college, and it determined the path he would then choose, a choice that would become for him both a source of great pride and a stigma. Around the time of Gil's sophomore year at UCLA, a schism developed between the UFW, headed by Cesar Chavez, and CASA, Bert Corona's organization. In the early 1970s, in an attempt to align itself with the AFL-CIO, the largest federation of unions in the country, the UFW had articulated its support for certain anti-immigrant positions that recommended using deportation as a measure to protect Mexican American workers against the perceived threat posed by Mexican immigrant workers. There were reports of some UFW members patrolling the border, on the lookout for undocumented immigrants they could somehow detain and hand over to immigration authorities. In staunch opposition to this, Corona publicly criticized Chavez at a press conference in Tijuana, calling him "irresponsible." Corona's comments were published in newspapers on both sides of the border, the story caught fire, and the UFW counterattacked. But the UFW also suffered the first political schism within its ranks, when half of its directors resigned.

This was a turning point for a young Gil. He was twenty and had witnessed firsthand the confrontation between the Chicano movement, a struggle fueled by his generation, and the calculating analysis of the working class.

"For me, as the grandson of an undocumented immigrant, between a position supporting the working class or the immigrant community, the choice was obvious. That was my destiny for the rest of my life. My politics have not changed since then."

In later years, Gil has learned how to navigate the political waters while waving the flag for immigrant rights. Some who were aligned with CASA think Gil has not been radical enough, while, of course, other groups feel he has not formed close enough ties with the Chicano elite. One of the most memorable instances of discord occurred during the launch of Antonio Villaraigosa's 2005 mayoral campaign, when Gil threw his support behind the opposing candidate, then-mayor James Hahn. Villaraigosa paid him back in kind years later, when Cedillo ran for a seat in the US Congress: Mayor Villaraigosa endorsed the Chinese American candidate Judy Chu, who won the election. In spite of these scuffles, Gil Cedillo, the pro-immigrant politician, activist, and Chicano, is generally widely supported.

IN 2004, WHEN I BEGAN working as a reporter for *La Opinion*, I was assigned a story that had to do with Gil Cedillo. I had been in Los Angeles for only a short time and was still unfamiliar with the political landscape in California, so I asked one of my colleagues who he was. "He's the driver's license guy," he said simply. In 1998, as a state assemblyman, Gil introduced a bill that would grant driver's licenses to undocumented immigrants. Aside from authorizing people to drive, in the United States, driver's licenses also function as the most widespread form of official identification. Those in favor of the legislation assert that letting everyone apply for a license would not only improve undocumented immigrants' quality of life by giving them access to better cars for transportation, which would be a boon to the automotive industry, it would also improve safety on the roads. Everyone knows what actually goes on now: out of sheer necessity, undocumented immigrants drive without licenses and buy cheap cars in poor condition because they know that if they get pulled over, their car will be confiscated and they'll have no way to recover it, so what's the point of investing a lot of money in a nice one? Licensed drivers can also get auto insurance policies that cover third parties, while undocumented immigrants cannot. Those against the measure argue that granting licenses to people in the country illegally poses a risk, since it would allow them to board a plane, open a bank account, register to vote, and take advantage of other privileges that are available only to legal residents.

Just as with California's version of the DREAM Act, the driver's license initiative has been introduced in the state legislature over and over again, eleven times in total. It was approved by the legislature several times, only to be vetoed by Governor Schwarzenegger. At other times it has not passed because of the political situation at that moment, or has been rejected because of the wording of certain passages, or because of the composition of the legislature along party lines. Governor Gray Davis did sign the bill into law in 2003, but the legislature rescinded it after Davis was recalled and Schwarzenegger took power. For fifteen years Gil Cedillo fought to get his initiative approved. Finally, on October 3, 2013, Governor Jerry Brown signed the law in front of the Los Angeles City Hall. At that moment, Cedillo was not an assembly member anymore; he was a member of the Los Angeles City Council.

AFTER WE STOOD talking in his office for a while, Gil invited me to sit down. A videographer named Hector was going to take some footage of our conversation, to use as B-roll for his documentary. Gil put on a navy-blue suit jacket and combed his hair. Hector went around straightening up the bookcases and rearranging things so that the most prominent piece of artwork in the background was the image of the Dreamers. This visual drove home the message that, over the past few months, Gil had gone from being "the license guy" to "the DREAM Act guy."

"Basically, this law says that we will accept the presence of undocumented students who were brought here through no choice of their own and who have played by the rules; it would require them to go to school and would allow us to assist the state's institutions of higher education, providing them with scholarships to be awarded to all the students in California no matter their legal status, race, age, color, or ethnicity," Gil explained in a much more formal tone than he had used thus far, no doubt because of the presence of the video camera.

Gil talked about California's history as a leader in promoting social justice movements. Sounding like the lawyer he is, he referred to *Brown v. Board of Education*, the 1954 Supreme Court decision that represented a watershed moment in the civil rights struggle, establishing that segregating black students from white students in schools was unconstitutional. A similar case had preceded that one in Orange County, California, eight years earlier, when a federal court ruled in *Mendez v. Westminster School District* that segregating Mexican and Mexican American students from the general school population violated the constitution. Building on those precedents, the Supreme Court in 1982 in *Plyler v. Doe* struck down a Texas law that had barred undocumented immigrant children from receiving a public secondary school education, from kindergarten through twelfth grade, and established that any child has the right to an education, regardless of immigration status. In California in 1994, voters passed Proposition 187, which intended to rescind that right to a public education and to deny undocumented immigrants access to public health and human services. But once again, higher courts struck down the measure.

The last judicial link in the chain of the struggle for immigrant rights and California's DREAM Act is Law AB 540, legislation introduced by Marco Antonio Firebaugh. Born in Tijuana, Firebaugh was a California state assemblyman from 1998 until 2004. With a slender build, clean-shaven face, and wire-framed glasses and with eyes that crinkled almost shut when he flashed his bright smile, he was one of the most vocal supporters of equal access to education for undocumented students. In 2001 he presented his initiative, which would establish that students who had graduated from high school in California could pay in-state tuition at state universities, even if they did not have a document proving their residency, instead of having to pay the much higher tuition rate for out-of-state students. This law would mean the difference between going to college or not for undocumented students with limited financial resources. At the University of California, for example, which includes UCLA, annual in-state tuition is $13,200, while out-of-state tuition is $36,000.

AB 540 was passed in September 2001, signed into law by Governor Gray Davis a month later, and went into effect in January 2002. With its passage, California joined Texas, which in 2001 became the first state to pass a law allowing undocumented students to pay in-state tuition. In 2002 Utah and New York passed their own laws, and they were later followed by Washington, Oklahoma, Illinois, Kansas, and Nebraska. New Mexico did not pass a state law but adjusted the requirements of some of its universities so undocumented students can qualify for in-state tuition and compete for financial aid. Other states, including Colorado, Connecticut, Florida, Hawaii, Massachusetts, Minnesota, New Hampshire, New Jersey, North Carolina, South Carolina, Oregon, Tennessee, and Virginia, have legislation pending. In contrast, Arizona and Georgia have modified their laws to explicitly prohibit any kind of tuition adjustment that would benefit undocumented students.

In 2006, Firebaugh died of liver disease. He was only thirty-nine. Now an entire generation of students will be forever grateful to Firebaugh for fighting for their right to an education.

The next link in the chain for California was the DREAM Act.

Gil positioned the initiative as a precedent that would lay the foundation for similar acts of legislation across the country, as has occurred before. He said this without a trace of arrogance. It seemed as if even though he understood it would be a huge accomplishment, it was the least that he expected of himself. While Gil talked about the role his initiative had played in pushing forward legislation in other states, Hector, a dark-haired man in his forties who spoke to me deferentially in Spanish, carefully captured Gil's words and gestures on camera, as if he had determined this was the crucial section that had to be included in his footage. Hector's assistant, a nicely dressed young woman, took photos of Gil, of Hector filming Gil, and of Gil and me talking. Gil projected a natural air, leaning forward when he wanted to emphasize a point, and then sitting back in a more relaxed posture. I was impressed by how calm his gaze was the whole time, punctuated by warm smiles that put everyone around him at ease. He was a politician, after all.

Our conversation moved on to federal politics. The California DREAM Act would open a door to higher education for undocumented students, but it would not provide a solution for the underlying issue: these immigrants still could not legalize their status, and they had no path to US citizenship.

Gil told me that his initiative had already prompted changes in Washington. He said it had served as motivation for President Obama to announce that students would not be subject to deportation and to implement the Deferred Action program. "I think it will have an effect at the global level, too," he said. "These students are part of different diasporas, different movements around the world, in a global economy. People come to the United States in search of a better life, so it's not just Mexicans, Latin Americans, or Asians who may be the most visible but Europeans and Africans, too. We are having an impact there as well. We've gotten reports that in Ethiopia, the media ran stories about the California DREAM Act and the way we're welcoming these young men and women. It's not just an important initiative for this country but for the whole world."

Then I asked if he really thought that if Obama was reelected, the DREAM Act might pass. By this point Hector had stopped filming and had packed up his video camera. Gil leaned a little closer toward me, changed his tone of voice, and stared intently into my eyes as he spoke, as if to ensure that I got every single word.

"We will try to be considerate and to respect the views of the opposition," he said, trying to state this as politely as possible. "Obviously many Americans are afraid of losing the advantage that they have, but there is no valid reason to punish young men and women who came here through no choice of their own, not speaking the language, and who in a short time have adopted our values, have met our standards and exceed our expectations. These young people become the students who graduate with honors, who win scholarships; there's no reason to punish them just because they're struggling to get ahead in the economy we have right now. I believe these workers will be a part of our intellectual capital, of our future work force. They will be innovators, business owners, scientists, doctors, engineers, political leaders. They will be what California and this country needs to maintain our position in the global economy."

Then he told me a story about how a very angry man had once called him at his office and asked why Gil was helping "those people." "Because I believe Californians and Americans deserve the best," he had replied. And he had given an example. "If your wife got sick, and you found out she has a brain tumor, wouldn't you want her to get the very best care? Wouldn't you want the head of brain surgery at Johns Hopkins, the best hospital in the field, to be her doctor?" The caller had said of course he would. "Well, that doctor, who is one of the very best in the country today, was at one time an undocumented immigrant."

Gil was talking about Dr. Alfredo Quiñones Hinojosa. Ever since the debate over legalizing undocumented students entered the national spotlight, Dr. Quiñones has participated in panel discussions and given television interviews, explaining how the very same hands that had once picked tomatoes in the fields in California when he was an undocumented worker are now saving lives, operating on the most exquisitely delicate organ in the human body.

Dr. Quiñones, now forty-six, was originally from Mexicali, Mexico. He began working at his father's gas station when he was only five, a precarious situation that only got worse when the business failed. At nineteen he decided to emigrate to the United States, climbing over the border fence. He began working in the fields, living in a ramshackle mobile home. He held down a series of jobs, whatever he could get while he saved money to go to school at night. He finally won a scholarship to attend the University of California, Berkeley, and from there went on to Harvard Medical School. Twenty years later, he is one of the most respected doctors in his field. Dr. Quiñones is short and stocky, with a dark complexion, straight nose, square jaw, and a warm expression and wears round, plastic-framed glasses. From his office at Johns Hopkins

Medical Center, in his lilting accent, he tells interviewers about his journey from undocumented field worker to surgeon with his own operating room in one of the most renowned hospitals in the world. His critically acclaimed memoir, *Becoming Dr. Q*, was published in 2011 by the University of California Press.

"That's why I do it," says Gil about the story of Quiñones. "I don't want us to miss out on the opportunity to have the very best this country could offer us. These kids are brilliant. Every day they are bombarded with hate on the radio and television, and in spite of poverty, and the huge obstacles in their way, they rise to meet the challenge. They learn the language, work, and pay for school. They've become the best this country has to offer, and we should recognize that and encourage them."

GIL CEDILLO'S POLITICAL capital lies in his tireless struggle for immigrants' rights. Over the course of the fifteen years he has worked in both houses of California's legislature, most of the bills he has presented have been related to immigrants' rights. This has been a double-edged sword, on the one hand assuring him a solid base of supporters throughout the state and bolstering his image as a politician with convictions, true to his ideals. But his unwavering fight on the issue also makes him the perfect target for conservative groups. Some of his opponents call him "One-bill Gil."

Gil Cedillo was one of the first Latino politicians to openly support Barack Obama's bid for the presidency, and he actively campaigned for Obama in 2008 in California, Texas, and Nevada. He brought a truckload full of volunteers with him to Nevada, where they campaigned for Obama for five days. Gil threw his support behind Obama because he believed comprehensive immigration reform had an excellent chance of getting passed if he were elected. But not only did that not take place during Obama's first term, as president he earned his reputation as the "Deporter in Chief."

"I have as much right to be disappointed as any other immigrant does," Gil tells me, with no trace of a smile. "He told me personally that there would be a reform, and instead of that, he deported more people than ever before. Look—" He leaned in closer, as if to tell me a secret. "I've been fortunate. Because of all the early support I gave him, he's invited me to meetings and private parties. I've used these opportunities to remind him of his promise and to tell him what he's doing isn't why we campaigned for him. It's not what we talked about, and he has to stop it. Maybe that's why I don't get as many invitations as I used to. The last time he told me he was working on it, that he's done the best that he could, that it's hard, there's a lot of opposition. But none of those answers are adequate."

Still, Gil believes that Deferred Action is a step forward. It's a message Obama sent to the community, to let them know he has not forgotten his promise. Gil believed the federal DREAM Act could pass in Obama's second term, and maybe even comprehensive immigration reform.

"We needed something fast, Deferred Action, the California DREAM Act, something to give us the strength to keep going," said Gil. "We needed a win, because the failure of the DREAM Act in 2010 was really hard for students. They're so young and so full of hope; they have no experience with failure. They thought they were going to win in 2010; it didn't happen, so they were devastated. That's why the California DREAM Act is so important for the rest of the country. The people need a reason to hope, and you can't hope if you always lose."

While Gil talked about how he had bet on Obama, he remembered the day he had publicly announced he was supporting Governor Jerry Brown. It was an afternoon in July 2010, at the height of summer in Los Angeles. That day, as a reporter, I had been covering an event where all the most prominent Latino leaders of the state were gathered, at an esplanade on the UCLA campus. State senators, assemblymen, and council members symbolically closed ranks around one man: the candidate for governor, Jerry Brown. Naturally, Gil Cedillo was there.

As my conversation with Gil drew to a close, I reminded him of that event and of how, with Brown's victory, there had been a new, very real possibility of passing the California DREAM Act.

Gil reminded me that 11 percent of the votes cast for Brown were from Latinos, "immigrants who speak English, who are new citizens, newly registered to vote, with the intention of overcoming anti-immigrant sentiment, and that was the margin of victory for the governor."

I asked him to tell me about the first time he spoke to Brown about the DREAM Act. Gil chuckled and averted his eyes. He paused for a long minute and then, still smiling, met my gaze with his big, brown eyes, with the permanent dark circles underneath. He seemed to be trying to come across as sincerely as he could.

"I'm going to tell you the truth," he said. "I tried not to talk about it with Brown so I wouldn't get a negative response. I listened to what he said; I watched the debate between the two candidates. I saw when a woman stood up and asked Meg Whitman what she would do about all the undocumented students, and Whitman answered that she would deport them all. And then Brown got up and said he wouldn't, and that he would sign the DREAM Act. When somebody says that, I accept it; I don't question it. I took them at their word and tr[ied] to hold them to it. So we really didn't talk about it beyond what he said publicly."

Gil says he never contacted Brown, but he did work hard on his campaign. And when he was elected, Brown kept his word. I asked Gil to tell me about the ceremony held at the library of the Los Angeles City College, where Brown signed into law the first part of the DREAM Act after it had been passed in both chambers of the state legislature.

Gil beamed his brightest smile, which reminded me of how he looked the evening he was honored at the CHIRLA gala. It's the same smile he flashed whenever he talked about the young people who work in his office as interns, a classification that allows some undocumented youth to be a part of his team. He leaned back, relaxed again.

"We were very focused on capturing the moment that day, because we knew it was historic," he said. "We knew the world would be watching us, and it was important to us to present images that reflected the event's importance. I was super happy. I always am, but that day I tried to concentrate on all the details. We knew that anti-immigrant groups might protest, so we had to have security in place. At the same time we didn't want people to think these kids were getting something that would be denied to their kids. It was very important to us that everyone understand that. The event was on a Monday, so the Saturday before we had gone to the venue and worked on the logistics so everything would be perfect . . . even though in the end not everything went according to plan," he says with a laugh.

In the morning on July 25, 2011, Brown arrived at Los Angeles Community College, where dozens of students, officials, and reporters enthusiastically awaited him, and the ceremony began. Some young students served as masters of ceremonies, and a couple gave speeches, as did Gil and Governor Brown. When it came time for Governor Brown to sign the bill into law, photographers discovered that with everyone standing, the cameras couldn't see Brown sitting at the desk. So in a poetic moment of improvisation, Brown stood, asked Gil to lean over a bit, and signed the California DREAM Act into law on Gil's back.

CHAPTER SIX

◆

DREAMING IN ARIZONA

*The future belongs to those who believe
in the beauty of their dreams.*

—ELEANOR ROOSEVELT

THIRTY RIOT POLICE STOOD in a line along the street in front of a high school in Phoenix, Arizona. It was six o'clock in the evening on March 20, 2012, and the sun had just begun to dip below the horizon. After ten minutes of standing stock-still, awaiting orders, suddenly they took a step toward the protesters on the other side of the street. For an instant, the sound of their polished boots meeting the pavement overshadowed everything else. It wasn't a constant, rhythmic sound. It was a single *crack!* as their feet hit the ground in front of them; they were wearing bulletproof vests, carrying batons and handcuffs, staring straight ahead. *Crack!* Two minutes of standing completely still, silent; then another step. *Crack!* Helmets with protective shields over their faces, leather gloves. *Crack!* Rounds of ammunition, firearms. *Crack!*

A few yards in front of the advancing riot police six young undocumented immigrants sat on a blanket in the middle of the street, blocking Thomas Avenue in West Phoenix, the city's Latino neighborhood. The black T-shirts they wore declared in bold red letters they were "Unafraid," with the tagline underneath adding, "We will no longer remain in the shadows." They also voiced this message out loud, shouting it out with fists raised in the air, defiant, in a direct challenge to the local police in riot gear and the infamous sheriff of Maricopa County, Joe Arpaio. Passing a megaphone back and forth, they declared their willingness to go to jail, to face immigration authorities, and to run the risk of being deported. Jackie, an eighteen-year-old girl with a dark complexion and black hair, sat with her long legs crossed. Her back straight, she raised her arms in the air in a show of protest and watched wide-eyed as the shiny police boots advanced, one step at a time. Rocio, seventeen, was next to her. With hair bleached almost white, wearing oversized glasses, Rocio let out a laugh, a nervous giggle that seemed to say, well, there's no turning back now. Then there was Daniela, twenty years old, wearing tight jeans and white sneakers with "Dream" written on them. She managed to keep smiling and put on a strong front all day, until the police made their move. Then she turned to look at the people watching them from the sidewalk, as if removing the line of riot police from her field of vision might somehow halt their advance. Viridiana, also twenty, seemed the most stoic of them all, and also smiled the least. Just before the police began to move, the tears won out as her mother approached to quickly wrap her in a supportive hug. But moments later she recovered her hardened stance as the sound of boots echoed against the pavement, her eyes fixed in a warrior's gaze.

The six protesters had undergone several days of training to prepare for this moment. To reach this point, they had had to learn the meaning of civil disobedience. They learned the police would order them to get out of the street since they were blocking traffic. They would not comply, and they would continue chanting slogans along with the hundred or so supporters who would be there with them. Then, they learned, the police would surely call for reinforcements. The reinforcements would arrive in two trucks, which would stop right in front of them. Then the police would give them a final warning and order them to leave the street, a warning they would ignore. Then thirty police in riot gear would line up across the street, forming a wall, and start their intimidating march toward them: *Crack!* Then a moment's pause, then another step—*crack!*—with their noisy boots. The protesters learned the inevitable moment would come when those boots would be right in front of their faces. They would still sit there, the six of them, their fists raised in the air, shouting, "*Undocumented and unafraid!*"

The city of Phoenix wasn't particularly surprised by protests anymore. Undocumented immigrants are always there, even if you don't see them, and sometimes they are scared to death. They try to go out as little as possible and avoid attracting unnecessary attention. But ever since 2006, when the anti-immigrant bill HR 4437—also known as the Sensenbrenner law, after the congressman who introduced it, and which would have made unlawful presence in the United States a felony—provoked marches and protests in dozens of cities across the country, immigrants living in Phoenix know that there are days when they must get up their courage, gather their families together, and take to the streets. And one by one, their numbers have added up to more than a hundred thousand.

Of all the protests that have taken place in Phoenix in recent years, one in early 2010 stands out from the rest. That march was not protesting proposed federal legislation, like the Sensenbrenner law, or a state law, like SB 1070, known as the Arizona law. It wasn't even against a particular government agency. This march was held to protest one particular person, a man who possesses the uncanny ability to inspire admiration and affection in some and disdain and virulent hatred in others: the Maricopa County sheriff, Joe Arpaio.

Joseph M. Arpaio was born in 1932 in Springfield, Massachusetts, the son of Italian immigrants. His mother died giving birth, and little Joe was raised by his father, who owned a small grocery store. At eighteen he enlisted in the Army, just before the Korean war broke out. He was stationed in France for a time and served in the Medical Detachment Division. In later years he worked as a policeman in Washington, DC, and Las Vegas. The stories told about him from that time have the ring of legend: he was known for never conceding in a fight, and once while working in Las Vegas, he pulled over a motorcyclist who turned out to be Elvis Presley, accompanied by a beautiful woman.

His next stop was the Federal Office of Narcotics, which later became known as the US Drug Enforcement Administration (DEA).

Over the thirty-two years Arpaio worked there, he was assigned to cases in Argentina, Turkey, and Mexico and eventually headed the DEA office in Arizona. He remained in that post until 1993, when he was elected sheriff of Maricopa County, which includes Phoenix. Arpaio has been elected to four-year terms five times, most recently in November 2012.

For almost twenty years, Arpaio, who calls himself "America's toughest sheriff," has sustained a ruthless campaign against undocumented immigrants with the goal of "wiping them out." A shameless publicity hound, he has created a constant persecution of undocumented immigrants that he proudly promotes, even appearing on the Fox reality show *Smile . . . You're Under Arrest*, in which he is shown in a segment arresting immigrants.

As a state that shares a border with Mexico and has a lackluster track record on civil rights, many anti-immigrant organizations are located in Arizona, including the Minutemen, self-styled vigilantes who see it as their mission to prevent undocumented immigrants from crossing the border into the United States. Arpaio is very popular among these groups and among the highest echelons of political conservatives, mostly white, who justify the steady stream of human rights violations the sheriff's agents commit on his behalf.

Bolstered by his supporters, Arpaio made it his mission to train his staff in how to effectively harass and intimidate Phoenix's largely Latino immigrant community, with no regard to legal protections afforded to this country's residents meant to ensure that local authorities do not function as federal immigration agents. In Arpaio's jurisdiction, anyone who looks Latino can get stopped for any reason, whether it's for a broken tail light or acting "suspiciously." The police will demand to see identification proving they are residing in the United States legally. If they cannot produce this identification, they are detained and put into deportation proceedings. The Arizona and Alabama laws passed in recent years targeting immigrants have sought to make this practice explicitly legal. In both cases, the Supreme Court suspended that provision, but that has done nothing to deter Arpaio, who continues his crusade.

This practice basically went unnoticed by the media until February 4, 2009, when a startling image appeared on evening news broadcasts: 220 undocumented immigrants were shown shuffling along the streets of Phoenix, two by two, all shackled to a single long chain, wearing humiliating black-and-white striped prison uniforms, straight out of a cartoon. Under their striped uniforms, the bright pink underwear that Arpaio had forced them to wear visibly peaked through. All of the detained were men, whose criminal threat rested entirely in the fact that at some point they had managed to enter or remain inside the United States illegally. They were not convicted felons—murderers or bank robbers or gang members—just everyday immigrants who were arrested only because they could not produce a piece of paper when *la migra*, in this case the local police, stopped them. Those were the men subjected to this very public humiliation.

These prisoners were being transferred to an installation called Tent City, a concept dreamed up by Arpaio and inspired by the Army camps he had seen during the Korean war. Given the large number of immigrants detained by his officers, and reasoning that these people were not citizens but were nevertheless "enjoying" public services on the taxpayers' dime, the sheriff decided to create Tent City to house them. Enclosed by an electrified fence, the prisoners live outside with only tents for shelter, wearing their pink underwear.

"It was a circus. He gave the order, and the animals walked out of their cages," Alfredo Gutierrez, a journalist for the website *La Frontera Times*, told me over the phone, describing the march of the prisoners through the city in February 2009. Carrying their standard-issue prison blankets, the 220 men paraded down Gibson Street, shackled together in pairs, like a chain gang.

Before this staged event, Arpaio had summoned all the media, even making arrangements so reporters could watch the show from their parked cars. Although chain gangs had been largely condemned and phased out of the prison system completely by the 1950s, Arpaio strove to revive this barbaric practice, showing exactly how he thought the immigrant labor force in the United States deserved to be treated, a class of workers who continue to make their way to this country no matter how "tough" Arpaio may be.

In spite of how cruel and grotesque Arpaio's actions may seem, his solid support among voters has not wavered: he won 55 percent of the vote in the 2008 election. The same day that America elected its first African American president, Sheriff Arpaio won his race with a comfortable majority, giving him a mandate to continue treating minorities as slaves were treated more than a century ago.

But not everyone stands behind Arpaio. Between 2004 and 2007, almost 2,700 lawsuits were filed against him for civil rights violations, racial profiling, and other charges. In April 2008 the mayor of Phoenix, Phil Gordon, sent a letter to the Department of Justice and the FBI requesting that they investigate Arpaio for these allegations. Then in 2011, reacting to a Department of Justice report that found Arpaio's practices unconstitutional, the Department of Homeland Security revoked Sheriff Arpaio's authority to identify and detain undocumented immigrants. In 2012, the Department of Justice filed suit against Arpaio because he had not altered his department's practices of targeting immigrants in the slightest.

The troubling status quo in Phoenix has provoked action from federal authorities, as well as outrage among activists and the general public. In fact, the protest held in Phoenix on January 16, 2010, was not against the federal government or the state of Arizona but against Sheriff Arpaio himself. The day before, a caravan of activists and Arpaio opponents left Los Angeles, heading for Phoenix to join the protest. As a reporter covering immigration issues, I had been at the protests in Phoenix in 2006 and had written about the abuses perpetrated by Arpaio during his reelection campaign in 2008. Naturally I joined the Los Angeles contingent for this latest protest, arriving in Phoenix the night before.

The next morning, the weather was perfect for a protest. It wasn't cold and the Arizona desert sun that blazes and burns in the summer provided just enough warmth to make it comfortable. Very early, people began to gather in Falcon Park, in the southeast of the city, where the protest would take place. Most were Latinos, many of them undocumented and many accompanied by their children who were United States citizens. There were also people of all races and backgrounds, from as far away as Los Angeles and Chicago, who had traveled to march in solidarity with this immigrant community, suffering under the lash of racism wielded by Arpaio.

The crowd of almost ten thousand, a rare sight for Arizona's capital, was led by a group of Aztec dancers. The deep, solemn sound of a conch horn echoed through the air. The crowd instantly fell silent, and the march began. Only the bells around the dancers' ankles could be heard jingling along to the shell horn's strong, sustained note. It was very moving. The police officers acting as security for the march—from the city of Phoenix's police department, not under Sheriff Arpaio's jurisdiction—tried to contain their emotion. Those marching who had Aztec blood running through their own veins could not hold back their tears.

The march made its way down Thirty-Fifth Street, continuing for two miles to Tent City, next to the Maricopa County Jail. At times the mood was of anger and indignation, at others it was joyfully festive as singing and dancing took over. People lining the streets to watch as the marchers passed by clapped and nodded in support. Some stepped off the curb and joined in. In contrast with the pro-immigrant marches held in Phoenix in 2006, this time I didn't see any scuffles break out, and I didn't hear any of the anti-immigrant contingents who often show up to these sorts of events shouting, "Go back to your country!" The signs the marchers held aloft did most of the talking, many of them pointing out Arpaio's horrible memory. "Your parents were immigrants too!" one proclaimed. One group of young people talked about how European immigrants had arrived here and the right that Native Americans had to this land. The angry shouts a woman's voice hurled in the direction of the Sheriff's Office ("Fuck you! *Fuck yoouuu*, ARPAIO!" she yelled) blended with the song of the Los Angeles band Los Jornaleros del Norte:

> *Pero la raza es fregona*
> *Se las saben toditas,*
> *Si nos sacan por la tarde*
> *Regresamos de mañanita.*

But our people are strong,
Everybody would say,
If they kick us out in the afternoon
We'll be back the next day.

"Don't take my parents away," read a sign carried by a little girl. "Arpayaso," said another, playing on the Spanish word for clown, *payaso*. "Assassinate Arpaio," one sign declared. The march wrapped up with one shared hope on everyone's mind: that after years of impunity, the federal lawsuits against the sheriff would leave him destitute and possibly even behind bars himself. That thought made a woman near me smile, as she turned to proudly show me her sign: "*De rosado y anaranjado te he de ver, desgraciado!*" ("I'll see you in pink and orange, pig!")

AMONG ALL THE DREAMERS I HAVE MET, Viridiana Hernandez has one of the strongest presences. Slender, with a dark complexion, her black hair and dark eyes contrasting with her bright smile, Viri, as her friends call her, embodies all the youthful happiness of a typical twenty-year-old with all the frustration of someone who has been swimming against the current for nineteen of those years.

Originally from Jojutla, in the Mexican state of Morelos, Viri arrived in Arizona as a baby when her mother decided to risk it all to give her daughter a better life. Her parents, Viri's grandparents, were already living in the United States legally, thanks to the Bracero program, an agreement between the governments of Mexico and the United States to allow temporary contracted laborers coming from the first country to the second. Viri's mother could not join them legally because of age limitations established in the law regarding the children of Braceros, so she crossed the border illegally and arrived in Phoenix with her baby daughter.

Like so many other Dreamers, Viridiana has no idea what things are like where she was born. Sometimes her grandparents show her photos of Morelos after they have gone for a visit there and ask her,

"Do you remember this?" while showing her a place or a relative. Viri laughs. "How could I remember if I was only one?"

She adds, "I always knew I was from Mexico, but your family tells you not to tell anybody. I never knew what being Mexican really meant. I thought it was something bad, so I always would say I was born in Phoenix. One day at school, some kids started saying, 'I was born in this hospital. Oh, I was born in that one,' and I thought, 'Uh-oh.' I didn't know what to say, so I changed the subject, because I thought it would be bad to say you weren't from here."

Viridiana and I spoke in her family's living room in a house like hundreds of others in West Phoenix, a heavily Latino neighborhood. She sat on the sofa against the far wall, her long hair worn up and her carefully made-up face bathed in sunlight streaming in from the front window. Family photos lined the wall leading into a spacious dining room. As I looked around, two things in particular caught my eye: a large piñata suspended from the ceiling in the center of the house and, outside in the backyard, a large "bounce house," an inflatable structure that is a fixture at children's birthday parties for kids to jump around in, this one decorated with Disney princess characters. Viridiana explained that both items were part of their family business: her mother rented out the bounce house and sold piñatas.

Growing up Viridiana had a relatively normal childhood and adolescence, until she reached the grim turning point that all Dreamers must face: applying to college. She knew she was undocumented, but she learned the full significance of what that meant when, like so many others, she tried to apply for scholarships and realized she did not have the required Social Security number. Still, she got up her courage and decided to talk to a guidance counselor, reveal her undocumented status, and ask for help. The counselor told her not to bother; her parents surely didn't have twenty thousand dollars a year to pay for full tuition with no financial aid and, anyway, what would be the point of going to college if she could not legally work once she graduated?

"I was crushed. I thought, why have I been working so hard all this time? For a while I even blamed my parents. I told them, 'Why did you even bring me here? Why did you do this to me?'"

Viridiana, who projects such strength, breaks down as she tells me this. She opens her eyes wide, trying to keep the tears welling up from spilling out, but finally she relaxes and lets them fall. She lets out a sob.

"I hurt my mother so much when I said that. She looked me in the eye and said she did it because we didn't have anything back there. I didn't know what I was saying when I said that to her, but after, knowing how much my relatives who are still there suffer—" She pauses, unable to stifle a sob. Then she looks up and goes on, "I know I have a beautiful life, and they came here for me. I was their only daughter, their only child. And when my mom found out what they had told me at school, she told me not to give up. 'You're going to quit just because of what some old guy says? No, we're going to find out how you can go to college.'"

Google became Viridiana's new best friend. She did searches for "how do undocumented immigrants go to school" and "private schools in Arizona" and ended up finding a college near where she lived to apply to. There, they treated her very differently from the way the guidance counselor had, even though she was the first undocumented student who had ever tried to apply, and helped her find private scholarships and grants from various organizations.

On top of that, she got some unexpected help from the community. When she was a high school student, Viridiana had begun offering free English classes to people who lived in the area. In 2010, as the Arizona law was being debated in the state legislature, Viridiana got involved with activist groups and learned why undocumented immigrants were so vulnerable. One important factor was being unable to speak English. So she decided to do something about it and began offering free English as a second language classes for adults. When it came time for her to try and go to college, her students took up a collection for her, helped her organize fund-raising events, and some of them even handed her cash once in a while. "Take it, my child, for gas money," they would say. "But obviously they helped me buy so much more than gas," she said, smiling at the memory, clearly touched by their generosity.

The Arizona law and Sheriff Arpaio's politics have made their mark on Viridiana's generation. In their teenage years, just as they prepared to enter adulthood, anti-immigrant fervor reached a fever pitch.

"Everything started with that law," said Viridiana. "When I found out what it was about, I thought, they're doing this to me, and I'm just sitting here not doing anything. I had never been aware of who the sheriff was or what he did, but when the campaign to pass the Arizona law got started, I went around the neighborhood knocking on doors, asking people how they felt about it. Most people around here are Latinos, and a lot of them are undocumented. When I knocked on the door, first they thought maybe somebody was there to arrest them. When they let me in, they told me their stories, crying, and I found out people are afraid of Arpaio, not just his tactics but afraid of *him*. They say they can hear his hatred for us in his voice. People in my family, my godparents, people I love very much are afraid of the sheriff, and now even when I see him I get creeped out."

Viridiana discovered that this fear has even greater consequences. It's common, for example, for people to not see any distinction between the sheriff's officers, who work for the county, and the local police, who are the authorities responsible for dealing with crimes within the city of Phoenix. So women who are victims of domestic violence or sex crimes do not press charges, fearing that if they go to the police, they themselves could wind up being arrested just for being undocumented.

A few months before my interview with Viri, two hundred officers from Sheriff Arpaio's staff and more than two hundred volunteers took part in one of the largest roundup operations he had ever orchestrated. The area they covered ran from Thirty-Fifth Street to Sixty-Seventh Avenue, where Viri lives. At the time she was giving ESL classes four times a week. She decided that the roundup would not put a halt to her classes, but her students started calling her to say they couldn't come because they were afraid they would get arrested. Viri had to cancel classes for two weeks. During that time, she decided to go door to door to tell people what they should do if they were arrested: do not say anything, keep quiet, demand a lawyer. That's how she met a woman living in her neighborhood who had a five-year-old daughter. The woman told Viri she had not enrolled her daughter in kindergarten because she was afraid she would be arrested when she took her to school. Because of her mother's fear, the little girl would miss a whole year of school.

"We're so afraid of the people who are supposed to be protecting us," Viri said, anguished. "They're the ones deciding what our lives will be like, and we console ourselves saying it could be worse, but why not do something to make it better?"

FOUR MONTHS AFTER the protest in Alabama where thirteen of them were arrested, I meet up with some DreamActivist members again, this time in Arizona. It was a Sunday, and Mohammad "Mo" Abdollahi was giving me a second interview, this time in Phoenix. Two days later, on March 20, this group would carry out the first civil disobedience action of 2012. Just as they had done in Alabama, the group would spend the time leading up to the protest training for their arrests.

Mo and I had arranged to meet early in the morning at a local office that one of the group's supporters had offered to let the DreamActivist protesters use to prepare. It was rainy and gray that morning, in contrast with Arizona's typical sun and blue skies. When I drove into the parking lot I saw a solitary figure, the hood of his sweatshirt covering his head, a backpack draped over his shoulder, waiting outside in the rain for the others to arrive. I had last seen Mo in Montgomery after the arrests. That day he had seemed larger than life, making statements to the media, moving energetically among the crowd and talking to people, seeming to be everywhere at once. With that image in mind, maybe that's why I was surprised to see this young man, who looked shorter than he really was, hunched over in the rain, waiting.

As Mo saw me approaching, he smiled and quickly explained why we were there, feeling the need to make a justification as we walked inside. The offices belonged to a political group, and the walls were covered with souvenirs and photos from election campaigns and other political memorabilia.

"I don't really feel comfortable, but they offered us this place since somebody in the group works registering voters, and we accepted. I don't like Republicans or Democrats; I don't like politicians. Look, how ironic," he said, gesturing toward a photo on the wall of Janet Napolitano, the ex-governor of Arizona and at the time the head of the Department of Homeland of Security, which oversees ICE, the immigration agency that processed the deportations of undocumented immigrants. Mo studied the photo for a moment and grimaced.

The young people taking part in the protest began to arrive. The group dynamic was very similar to what I had seen in Alabama, as they went around the room and everyone explained why they were taking part, although this time everybody lived in Phoenix and knew each other. Viridiana was the first to speak.

"One day they said Sheriff Arpaio was rounding people up in my neighborhood," she said. "Parents stopped taking their kids to school, my family was afraid to go out. Arpaio is terrorizing people who don't have papers with the threat of deportation. That's not his job. His job is to go after criminals, not people in the community. I'm sick of being persecuted."

Besides Viri, who acted as liaison between the local activists and Mo's group, there were five others who would take part in the civil disobedience action to follow the protest march: Jackie, Rocio, Daniela, Stephanie, and Hugo. It would be the first time any of them had engaged in civil disobedience.

Unlike the protesters in Alabama, the group in Arizona exuded a happiness that seemed almost unnatural under the circumstances. Maybe it was their youth, or maybe their light attitude was a function of having grown accustomed to living under the constant threat of being harassed and, worse, by a sheriff who seems to believe he is the king of the county. They joked around sarcastically about driver's licenses and deportations, in a way that sometimes made me wonder if they fully understood the implications of the risks they were about to face. But Mo fit right in with them and joked around, too, although sometimes he had to take charge and steer the group back to the serious matters at hand. Dressed in well-worn jeans, a T-shirt emblazoned with the word "Undocumented," and sandals, Mo sat on the carpet and began making a list. He asked everyone to give him examples of situations that frightened their families or neighbors or of things they could not do because they were undocumented. There was a pause as they ran out of ideas. "Come on, you guys live in Arizona! Give me something good," Mo chided, and everybody laughed.

The list helped them prepare for talking with the media. Next they moved on to the logistics. The protest was being planned so secretly that at times it was almost comical. The room let out a collective gasp of surprise when a stranger walked into the office, someone who apparently worked there and had decided to come in on a Sunday to get some things done. Mo and the others smiled politely at him, rearranged themselves a bit, and began speaking half in code. As with previous protest actions, it was critically important to ensure that the police did not get there before the protesters and potentially block their access to the street. So Mo reminded everyone that the media would be informed of the action only a few hours before it began.

As if they were planning a sophisticated military assault, with a map of the target location drawn on a blackboard with arrows pointing in different directions, the group reviewed what would happen the following day. The action would take place in front of a high school where seven in ten students were undocumented. That was the audience they wanted to reach: students in the process of figuring out what they would do after they graduated and who may not have known that they had options to help them go on to college. The group would loudly chant slogans as they marched to get the students' attention and invite them to support the protest. Then they would block off the street, sit on the pavement, and wait to be arrested, with the hope that after they were released from custody a few days later, the students who had seen them, their parents, and other members of the community would then understand they did have options and could stop being afraid.

A lawyer arrived toward the end of their training session. An older man with graying hair and a sober expression, he walked in unceremoniously and sat down at the head of the table where the group had been working. With a deep voice and speaking deliberately, he introduced himself. He had been working as an immigration lawyer for nearly twenty years in Arizona, and he had seen it all. He specialized in particularly difficult cases.

"When you're all in jail, I'll be here working hard to get you out," he said. "I'm not going to leave you alone. I know how to delay an undocumented person's deportation for as long as possible, and I say this because it is very likely that a process of deportation will be opened for you."

The lawyer explained that even though the arresting officers would be from the Phoenix Police Department, they would undoubtedly wind up under Arpaio's jurisdiction because there was only one jail in the county. And when an undocumented person comes under his jurisdiction, Arpaio always notifies immigration authorities. He told them that if a process of deportation was opened and they appealed, they could be released from jail as the appeal made its way through the courts, but that process could take as long as six years.

"You need to understand that even though you will be free during the appeals process, this could change your life because it will cause you a great deal of stress," the lawyer said gravely.

"But we've got that already," Vira said, smiling sarcastically. "Any one of us could get arrested tomorrow just walking to the store."

Mo reminded them that they could always change their minds at the last minute. Once again he reiterated the final goal of the action: that after they were taken to jail, the immigration authorities would get involved, just like they had planned in Alabama and at all the other DreamActivist protests. The closer they got to being deported, the bigger the impact their eventual release would have—and the stronger their message would be.

"With any luck, you'll all be in jail by five o'clock tomorrow," Mo said.

IT WAS ELEVEN IN THE MORNING on March 20 when I got to Pink Spot, an Internet café in downtown Phoenix that would serve as DreamActivist operational headquarters during the protest. Mo and the others, five people who had traveled to Arizona with him and some who had arrived from California the night before, waited for the Dreamers who would be protesting to get there after school. Even though they all knew they would be spending the night in jail, none of the protesters wanted to miss school that day. While everyone waited for their arrival, the *click-click-click* of typing could be heard from several laptops as press releases and invitations to various organizations were sent out.

The protesters taking part in the action were meeting at Viridiana's house at one o'clock in the afternoon. The six showed up there, along with family members, friends, some organizers, and supporters. The girls looked pretty. Two days before, they had worn their hair casually pulled back in ponytails and had worn no makeup, but now they had carefully applied their makeup and styled their hair, having followed Mo's advice. The night before, Mo had told them to be sure to smile when the police took their mug shots after they were arrested, because the media would publish those photos. We don't want people thinking we look like a bunch of criminals, he had said.

It was almost time to leave, and you could feel the tension rising in the air. The joking around and lightheartedness of a few days before was gone. The protesters solemnly made last-minute phone calls and arrangements. All six wore black T-shirts proclaiming they would no longer live in the shadows. They all forced smiles to mask their rising anxiety.

In the last moments they would be alone before leaving for the protest site, a young Bolivian man named Benito, who lives in

Indiana and travels with Mo, led the group in a traditional ritual. The six went into a bedroom with him and sat on the floor, forming a circle around a bunch of burning sage leaves. Benito told the group to close their eyes, relax, and connect with their ancestors as they remembered why they were there. He asked them to think about what it meant to be undocumented, and how they had crossed the border, and all the times they had had to lie. He asked them to think about all the people who had played important parts in their lives and to focus on who they were that day: a group of young people who would stand up to Arpaio and tell him, "We've had enough, and now we're going to fight."

Once they arrived at Thomas Avenue, they made their last-minute preparations. They went over the slogans they would use, wrote down on their arms the number of the hotline they would call from jail, and kissed and hugged their family members. Mo gave them one last reminder: "This is a peaceful protest. You have to be friendly with the police."

The protest got under way. Passersby stopped to watch what was going on. The long row of police boots inched closer: *Crack! Crack!* Six young people with their fists raised defiantly in the air, their voices raised as one as they sang: *We are the Dreamers, the mighty, mighty Dreamers . . .*

JOE ARPAIO'S OFFICE is on the nineteenth floor of the Wells Fargo building in downtown Phoenix. Off the elevator bank there's a set of glass doors with an intercom, and all visitors must be buzzed in. Once inside, there's a small reception area with three armchairs arranged around a coffee table with a lamp on it. The atmosphere is comfortable, yet intimidating. Maybe it was the wood-paneled walls that made the room seem dark, or the security camera hanging from a corner in the ceiling, or the sensation of being watched through the polarized glass wall that divided the reception area from the rest of the office.

As I waited, a man came in wearing a cowboy hat with a feather in it. His long gray hair was gathered in a ponytail, and he wore big gold rings on his fingers, a large belt buckle, and cowboy boots. He had come all the way from Wyoming for an appointment he had made three months earlier to meet the sheriff. He was surprised that I had just shown up without an appointment. A few minutes later, Arpaio's spokesperson came out with an answer for me: the sheriff was in the office, and he was very sorry but the sheriff did not wish to make any statement about the undocumented students who had been arrested a day earlier while performing an act of civil disobedience. The spokesperson then ushered the man from Wyoming inside, who looked over his shoulder at me, triumphant.

Arpaio knows that arresting the six protesters in West Phoenix will no doubt stir up controversy, but that's nothing new. He navigates comfortably in that familiar territory, overseeing roundups resulting in large-scale arrests and in undocumented immigrants being deported for the slightest cause. Meanwhile in Washington, DC, thousands of pages are filled with reports on the progress of all the federal lawsuits filed against him. That's why Dreamers carry out protests in states like Alabama, Arizona, and Georgia, where laws aggressively persecuting undocumented immigrants have passed. Maybe that's why at the height of the protest, Viridiana stood up, grabbed a megaphone, and shouted angrily, "You can stop looking for me, Arpaio! I'm not hiding anymore, I'm undocumented and I'm right here! Come arrest me!"

After arresting the protesters and taking them to jail, Arpaio's officers notified ICE that six undocumented immigrants had been detained. But immigration authorities chose to exercise their discretion and not respond since none of the six had criminal records. After imposing a fine for blocking the street, Arpaio had to release them. Two days later, the six stood outside of the county jail, holding up a large banner emblazoned with the words "Arpaio, you don't scare us." All six went home without any charges having been filed and without any personal identification beyond their faith in their people and in one another. And for now, that was enough.

CHAPTER SEVEN

——◆——

DYING FOR A DREAM

"NO ONE CALLS AT eight o'clock on a Sunday morning unless it is to give news that cannot wait. And news that cannot wait is always bad news." Paul Auster opens his first book, *The Invention of Solitude*, describing getting the phone call informing him of his father's death. Ever since I read it, that phrase has popped into my mind whenever the phone rings very early in the morning or late at night. We expect the worst, and during those drawn out seconds between the phone's first insistent ring and hearing the voice on the other end, your heart stops, and the whole world seems to grind to a halt.

On the morning of June 15, 2012, I flew to McAllen, Texas, with a connection in Dallas. I took off from the Los Angeles airport at six in the morning and arrived in Dallas Fort-Worth a little after ten, local time. I ran through the airport to make my connection, jumped onto the shuttle train connecting the terminals, and turned on my cell phone. As I went up an escalator, I heard the sound of several new messages landing in my voice mailbox: *click, click, click*. Something bad must have happened, I thought, it's barely eight o'clock in Los Angeles. I put the phone to my ear and with my heart in my throat began listening to the messages. I almost fell over: President Barack Obama had just announced through Janet Napolitano, secretary of the Department of Homeland Security, a program of Deferred Action for Childhood Arrivals. Using parameters very similar to those outlined in the DREAM Act, the Deferred Action program would grant Dreamers permission to work for a period of two years and a Social Security number, which would protect them from being deported during that time. The measure would not permanently resolve their immigration status, but in any case it was still extremely good news.

Rumors had begun circulating a few days earlier that the federal government would make some sort of announcement before the end of the week, but the news was even better than what many had hoped for. Students and their supporters were ecstatic, and a wave of euphoric celebration swept across the country. While on the flight to McAllen, for a while I felt the same giddy emotions that the 1.4 million students who could benefit from the program, some of whom I had been in close contact with over the past several months, must have been feeling.

I landed in McAllen, and as soon as I stepped outside of the airport I was enveloped by the heavy, humid heat so typical of the Rio Grande Valley. There's something about the sky in this part of the country, always a brilliant blue (except when a hurricane threatens), serving as a steady backdrop for the whimsical parade of clouds marching across during the day. Straight rows of palm trees stand beside roads and highways all along the one hundred miles of the Rio Grande, the natural border between the United States and Mexico in the southern extreme of Texas.

I rented a car and drove to Mission, twenty minutes to the east of McAllen. Mission is a small city at the river's edge, right on *la linea* (the line). Eighty thousand people live there; 85 percent are Latino. The per capita income is less than $13,000, far below the national average of $53,000. One in four residents lives below the poverty line. This figure rises to one in three for residents under eighteen years of age.

Route 83 begins at the edge of the Rio Grande at the Gulf of Mexico, goes up to Nuevo Laredo, and then heads due north through Texas, crossing through several states and finally reaching North Dakota's border with Canada. At its beginnings in southern Texas, Route 83 passes through Mission, connecting it with other cities in the area. Like most of the valley, the landscape along Route 83 consists of large tracts of lush, wild vegetation, some cultivated fields, a few isolated, humble little houses here and there, occasional turnoffs down dusty dirt roads, and one small church, then another. A little store or business sometimes pops up between the modest dwellings, but overall the landscape is dominated by wild fields, farm plots—Mission is the grapefruit capital, according to its website—and the bloodied remains of animals that have been run over dot the highway: dogs, cats, and larger animals like armadillos or badgers. Summer was about to begin, and the car's thermometer indicated it was 106 degrees as a light rain began to fall. The steamy atmosphere was oddly similar to that of Louisiana's bayou, where the silence could also suddenly be broken by a chorus of loudly chirping insects. It was as if Mission were not mere minutes away from cities with heavy cross-border traffic, like Brownsville and McAllen but lost in the underbrush of this Texas-style bayou.

As I approached my destination, the giddy excitement that Obama's announcement had inspired in me gave way to a bittersweet uneasiness. In *The Red Notebook*, Paul Auster, of the early morning phone calls, had written about coincidences. *The president just had to make that announcement today*, I thought. *The very day I'm going to see Joaquin's family.*

JOAQUIN LUNA LERMA KILLED himself the night after Thanksgiving. He was nineteen, in his senior year in high school, and had planned on studying engineering. He was a Dreamer.

"He was a special boy, if you had only known him . . ." Santa Lerma Mendoza said to me right after opening the door. She invited me inside the house and showed me one of the many pictures of her son she had on display. "He was going to do great things in life. But now . . ." Her voice broke.

Santa is sixty years old, and all the pain she has lived through shows plainly on her face. She has the dark complexion wrinkled by the sun of someone who has worked outside in the fields all her life. Her features are still faintly visible in the slackened skin of one who has experienced a sudden and dramatic weight loss, as if her gaunt face were not quite her own. Her hair is rapidly going gray at the roots. Her small eyes have a swollen look, suggesting she cries herself into a fitful sleep every night. A photo taken a few months before of Santa embracing her son Joaquin underscores the depth of her current pain: with her round face, dark hair, the same wire-framed glasses, and a satisfied smile, the woman staring out at me from the picture looks twenty years younger than the Santa standing before me.

Her story could be that of any other migrant worker. Originally from Miguel Aleman in the Mexican state of Tamaulipas, Santa came to the United States as a young woman to work in the fields and clean houses. She came to the Rio Grande Valley area twenty-five years ago, when her pay was five dollars a week. After that, she would go wherever the work was. Once the school year finished, the family would go off to the fields in Arkansas, Indiana, or Minnesota, and she cared for her children as best she could. Diyer, the oldest at thirty-five, works as a truck driver. Then there are Sonia, thirty-four; Nina, thirty-three; and Carlos, thirty. They all share the last name Mendoza. That was Santa's family for several years, until she met the man who would be Joaquin's father. In 1993 while she was visiting Tamaulipas, Joaquin was born in the city of Diaz Ordaz. When he was just four months old, baby Joaquin went over the border bridge in his mother's arms, arriving in Mission, where he lived all his life. A year later Jesus was born, and Santa's family was complete.

In spite of the difference in their ages, Nina was very close to her little brother Joaquin. Although my initial contact with the family was through a phone call with Santa, Nina took charge of setting up our interview, emphasizing that the information I came away with must be used "with good intentions." Since Joaquin's death, dozens of reporters have filed through this house with their notebooks, television cameras, and impertinent questions. Just before I arrived, a young man from a TV station had come to their house to get a reaction from the family about Obama's Deferred Action announcement. They have felt the pain of Joaquin's absence for months, but the passage of time has not lessened its impact, and his mother and sister still break down in tears whenever they talk about him.

"He was the baby of the family," Nina says. "I would sit in the rocking chair and sing lullabies to him until he fell asleep: '*Señora Santa Ana, por que llora el niño, por una manzana que se le ha perdido.*'"

Nina is slender, with dark hair and delicate features. She has a pretty smile, but her expression is usually serious. She tells stories about her brother in minute detail, as if she is trying to preserve him in the telling and not let his memory fade away. She mostly talks about the times they spent together on the weekends: making nachos and watching a movie on TV, Joaquin coming over to her house and Nina fixing him pancakes, or the time she made him one of his favorite beef dishes for dinner, not knowing she was serving him what would be his very last meal.

Joaquin grew up in a loving environment. Since they were constantly on the move, the family saw a good part of the country. Joaquin as a little boy smiles at me from a family photo album, playing with his little brother, Jesus, in a backyard, or in the snow, or by a swimming pool, or in a field. Then Joaquin is a little older, around ten, dressed in his karate uniform, earning his yellow belt—Santa points out that he would have earned his black belt next—turning toward the camera with his mother's eyes and that wide-open smile that melted the hearts of his brothers and sisters. He was always happy and did not fight with anyone; he was respectful and a good student. He was somewhat introverted and did not have many friends, but he did have a very active imagination. On some days he was a Power Ranger for the afternoon or he would put a kitchen pot on his head and morph into Mr. Freeze, one of Batman's archenemies. He liked to watch TV when he got home from school, and as a teenager he became interested in computers.

His siblings describe Joaquin as a thoughtful, hardworking boy. On Saturdays and Sundays, he would mow his neighbors' lawns to earn money. He belonged to a youth group at the Pentecostal church his family attended, where he would offer advice and guidance to younger kids. There was something about Joaquin that inspired trust. Maybe it was his innocent, boyish face, with a fair complexion contrasting with his dark hair, or his slender build, which became even thinner as he grew into a tall young man. He liked music, and when he learned to play the guitar he used it in his activities at the church and started playing in a group at services there. Other churches even took notice of his talents and invited him to play and sing for their congregations. Joaquin had no problem playing for other denominations, explaining that Jesus did not die for just one sect; He died for everyone.

In spite of the palpable grief that infused the Mendoza home, the atmosphere there was welcoming and warm. All of the siblings except for Sonia live in the same neighborhood, near their mother. Her house is down a dirt road, almost at the end, on a large plot of fenced land. Little dogs run around in the front yard, next to the driveway. When they first lived there, there was no house on the property, and they lived in a trailer home. By the time Joaquin was a teenager, their home was the trailer and two more rooms, constructed of cement, metal, and wood. Santa raised chickens on the land behind the house and tended fruit trees all around the property.

Santa takes off the padlocks and forcefully pushes open a gate, being careful not to let the dogs out. The first thing I see is the silver pickup truck in the driveway. It was Joaquin's; seven months after his death it is right where he left it. Walking past the truck I see the house, painted in cheerful colors. It's not the small trailer of years before but a real house. Santa explains that the transformation was thanks to Joaquin.

Joaquin had shown a real talent for drawing ever since he was a small boy. When one of his older friends at their church noticed this, he offered to teach Joaquin how to use graphic-design programs on the computer. Joaquin quickly became an expert and began creating simple designs, which gradually became more complex. When he felt ready to tackle a project in the real world, Joaquin told his mother, "We're going to finish this house." He was seventeen.

Santa shows me the parts of the house that Joaquin designed himself, like the small living room we're sitting in, with attractive detailing in the molding on the ceiling that runs through the rest of the house, including a lovely floral design in his mother's bedroom. Joaquin was also in charge of the kitchen, the bathroom, the selection of materials, and the color scheme. He chose pastel colors for the walls, and white for the ceilings. The construction was done in 2010, and Santa remembers how her son would get up very early in the mornings, in spite of the December cold, and get right to work, going all day and into the night. The house was inviting, attractive, and cozy, but Joaquin still saw things that he wanted to fix.

When Santa is around, the Mendoza family speaks Spanish, but among themselves her children mix English and Spanish. They mostly talk about Joaquin in the present tense, as if he were still with them and avoiding the past tense could keep him close, combatting the painful absence at the heart of their family.

In this part of Texas, you don't have to look hard to see two national cultures overlapping. There are the big corporations, like McDonald's and Target, but there are also smaller businesses showing their local colors, like a sign along the highway that reads "*Se venden borregos gordos para fiestas.*" ("We sell fat sheep for banquets.") The sign in front of the local school says "Emiliano Zapata Elementary School." Joaquin had attended Benito Juarez-Abraham Lincoln High School. That school has a total of 2,111 students: one is white, one is Native American, and 2,109 are Latino. Some 97 percent of those Latino students are categorized as "economically disadvantaged."

PAN AMERICAN IS ONE of the nine University of Texas campuses, located in Edinburg, about a half hour from Mission. To get there, you have to drive on a quintessentially Texan road that seems to be straight as an arrow forever, with palm trees and rugged fields on either side. It's easy to tell when you're getting close to the university campus, because the buildings change, the street layouts change, the air itself seems to be somehow loftier. Even though it's very close to the surrounding towns, it's clear that this academic enclave is a world unto itself.

As you drive through Edinburg, scrubby fields with trailer homes give way to apartment complexes and dorm buildings typical of an American university campus. Brick- and stucco-faced buildings appear along Sugar Avenue: the main library, the technology center, the computer studies building. A solar-powered parking garage for students, faculty, and visitors is on a side street, and beyond that are tennis courts and a football field. The grand buildings seem almost too large for the area when compared with the small houses just a few blocks away. The signs posted give an indication of the diverse areas of study at the university: Investigation and Innovation, Border Studies, Fine Arts. The impeccably manicured lawns do not seem to belong in this southern Texas landscape, with its oppressive heat. They look pampered and well tended, unlike the fields of wild vegetation in the surrounding area. But the calls of the birds native to the region, easily heard all around, provide a constant geographical reminder. At the center of the campus is a large cafeteria.

Summer vacation has just begun, and the campus is practically deserted. But there are signs posted on the cafeteria's walls that offer a glimpse of what student life is like during the semester. There are signs urging freshmen and sophomores to seek out academic mentors, with a picture of two young blonde women and a young man with dark hair, all stylishly dressed, attractive and smiling. There are posters lining a hallway from various Christian organizations, featuring more pictures of attractive young people enjoying themselves, inviting students to join their ranks. Then there is a scrappy little flier taped to the wall, barely noticeable, quietly offering an alternative: "Are you skeptical, agnostic, liberal, free-thinking, unorthodox, progressive, humanist, rational—" The question ends right there, because someone has torn the paper in half across the middle.

Joaquin had hoped to attend Pan Am. He wanted to be an architect or a civil engineer. He knew that because of his immigration status, he could not receive federal scholarships, but Texas allows its residents to benefit from some support provided by the state without having to demonstrate legal status. Nine in ten students at Pan Am are Latino, and some are undocumented. As in other states, community organizations have created financial aid alternatives for undocumented students, so that colleges and universities will have student bodies that reflect the local demographics as much as possible.

Just a few weeks before he died, Joaquin had completed the university's applications. He was also researching potential sources of financial assistance. He had found out about CAMP, a federal program that provides financial support for the first year of college for children of migrant workers or for migrant workers themselves who want to attend college. To apply for the program, Joaquin had to write a brief essay about his goals:

REALIZING A DREAM ON HOLD

My main goal is to become a successful architect and help my family however I can, just like they have always helped me and been there for me.

If I had the legal requirements to pursue my goal, nothing could stand in my way. I am confident that CAMP can help me to become the person I have always dreamed of being.

This would have a great impact on my whole family, especially my parents, who have struggled practically their whole lives. They have unconditionally supported me, just as they will support my brother.

I want to show my parents that all of the work they did in the fields, and all that time giving the best of themselves was worth it.

The possibility of becoming the first person in my family to earn a college degree makes me want it even more, since I want to prove to myself and to many other people that the fact that you do not have financial aid does not mean you have to give up going after what you have always wanted to do. That would make my dream complete.

A DAY AFTER I ARRIVED, I went back to the Mendoza house. Santa had been waiting for me since early in the morning. "If you come back tomorrow morning, I'll take you to visit Joaquin," she had told me the day before. Nina had left her children with a babysitter and came along with us. The Garden of Angels cemetery was a twenty-minute drive away, so we got going.

The number of churches is what stands out the most along the roads in the area. They represent a surprising variety of denominations—evangelical, missionary, Seventh-day Adventist, Presbyterian, Pentecostal—with names like Dios Salva or Jesus el Pan de Vida. The styles of the church buildings are as varied as the denominations. Some are so humble that without a sign out front, you wouldn't even know it was a church; others are larger, some with even more than one building—those have clearly been around the longest. There is a church every two blocks, or even on every block, tucked in next to the pet shops, thrift stores, building supply stores, fruit markets, and taco stands. While I was in Mission, I came across only one Catholic church, called San Juan Diego.

I remarked to Santa that there were a lot of different churches for such a small, not very densely populated city, and so many denominations. She told me about how her church community and the counseling her pastor had offered her had helped her to go on after she lost her son. "The smallest churches, where all the members know each other, are the most unified, because the pastor really talks to the people," she said.

Then our conversation turned back to Joaquin. Santa proudly talked about her son's spiritual life, about how familiar he was with The Word, and how much he enjoyed reading the Bible. He wasn't like those boys who go around "badly dressed." He had his work clothes for mowing lawns, but as soon as he was done, he would take a shower and put on a nice outfit. He liked to wear long-sleeved dress shirts and ties. Laughing, Nina interrupted her mother to tell me about how between the two of them, they figured out how to tie a tie knot—and how much attention he paid to his grooming and appearance. He was discreet and got along with everybody. He was a peacemaker, a natural diplomat who didn't want to hurt anyone's feelings. He listened to Christian radio and talked to people about his faith but did not try and force his beliefs on anyone. He had decided not to have a girlfriend.

"My son had seen how other boys let themselves give in to temptation, how they offended God," Santa said. "There is a lot of fornication in the world. This hurt him a great deal. Girls went after him, they passed him little notes that said, 'I love you,' but he never touched a girl because he said he wasn't ready to have a girlfriend. He would say to me, 'I'm going to be like Isaac. If I have a wife, it's going to be for my whole life.'"

"Did Joaquin have any flaws?" I asked.

"Taking his life," his mother answered.

The Garden of Angels cemetery sits on a huge plot of land. Like everything else in the area, it seems to be one with the crystalline blue sky and brilliantly white clouds. It is divided into two sections, one where large headstones and even little mausoleums are permitted and another with only small, horizontal headstones over the graves. Joaquin's grave is in the second section.

A few years earlier, Santa had purchased the cemetery plot, thinking that this way if anything happened to her, she would not place this burden on her children, especially Joaquin. Like any parent, she never imagined that one day she would be burying her son instead.

The headstone rests over two graves. Santa has already decided that when she dies, she will be buried next to her son, so her name is on the gravestone, too. On one side, Joaquin's date of birth, April 17, 1993, and the date of his death, November 25, 2011, are engraved below his name. Next to that, below Santa's name, is her date of birth, December 1, 1951, with a blank space next to it, where the date of her death will be engraved once she is buried there. "I pray to God, 'Please, take me now, take me to be with him,'" Santa says. "But He doesn't listen. He doesn't listen."

Nina remembers her brother's funeral. Still surprised by it all, she tells me how a steady stream of cars slowly drove into the cemetery and made their way to the burial plot, and dozens and dozens of high school kids got out of the cars, classmates from Joaquin's school, students from other schools, friends from church, teachers, neighbors, people who heard about his death in the news and wanted to show their support to the family. Joaquin's siblings had thought it would just be them and a few neighbors. They spent more than two hours there that day shaking the hands of everyone who had come to offer condolences.

We go back to Santa's house. There is a small altar in the bedroom that Joaquin designed for her, with a collage of photos and messages from Joaquin's classmates on it. On the bedroom walls hang some of the drawings and architecture plans that he had designed at school and photos of Joaquin with his family, hugging his mother, celebrating a birthday. A record of his baptism at church is prominently displayed on a book shelf, along with the diploma and graduation cap that were symbolically presented to Nina a few days before my visit, when the senior class at Juarez-Lincoln had their graduation ceremony. A poster given to the family features a photo of Joaquin and the caption "You don't need papers to get into heaven."

"I couldn't be without him," Santa says after a long silence. "The little that I had was because of him. Now I don't have anything."

Joaquin was buried on December 1, after the autopsy and necessary legal process following a suspected suicide were finally completed. As the silver-colored coffin was lowered into the ground, his mother sang a song about Pimpon, a doll made out of cardboard, just as she had sung to her beloved boy when he was a baby. Santa turned sixty the day she laid her son to rest.

DIYER MENDOZA IS A LARGE MAN with a strong presence. He speaks in a measured, firm tone. His black hair and mustache frame his dark-skinned face, marked by acne scars and browned by the sun. He has worked for years as a truck driver, traveling from one state to the next, and the next, loading up and unloading, and always on the road. Like his siblings, Diyer lives in Mission.

The day I said good-bye to the Mendozas, after we visited Joaquin's grave, I was packing up for my trip back to Los Angeles when I got a phone call. It was Diyer, calling from somewhere on the road. Nina had told him a journalist was writing about Joaquin, and Diyer insisted that we meet before I left. He would forgo a rest stop on his way back so he could arrive in Texas in time.

The next morning, I met the eldest of the Mendoza family. His wife and three children were with him when he showed up carrying a couple of boxes. "I have Joaquin's papers, his school papers, his drawings, his writing. I want to show you the letters he wrote before he died," Diyer said.

He started to take out papers, folders, and notebooks. One large envelope was stuffed with certificates and awards. Diyer showed them to me one by one, talking about each in detail at first, and then just laying them down on the table. There were almost thirty awards for Joaquin's academic achievements in math, science, and reading. There were also brochures from colleges and universities, including Pan Am. Some of his drawings had to do with architecture and design. Others had religious symbolism, such as a drawing of the Virgin of Guadalupe, composed of geometric figures painted in different colors. His writings tended to be brief, and many had religious overtones. In one, he mused about how it would be if everyone treated the Bible the way they treated their cell phone: if they never left home without it and always carried it in their pocket, consulting it several times a day. What if parents gave teenagers Bibles as presents, and what if everyone reached for their Bible first in case of an emergency. . . .

Diyer solemnly showed me a notebook with a red cover. Joaquin had written a series of letters saying good-bye to his family, and he had also written what would become known as his suicide note in it, in English.

Jesus Christ 11-25-11

Dear Lord forgive me for what I am about to do tonight. I know it has to be done because I have no point of existence in this cruel world. There are many problems going among teenagers these days and I am fearful to fall in any temptation. Jesus, I realize I have no chance of becoming a civil engineer the way I always dreamed of here. So I am planning in going to you and helping you construct the new Temple in Heaven.

There were more letters. One was to Diyer, telling him how sorry Joaquin was that he wouldn't be the first in the family to graduate from college and help him buy the best tractor-trailer out there. Joaquin wrote to his sisters, thanking them for all they had done for him and asking them to take good care of their children. He wrote a letter to his parents in Spanish, thanking them for all they had given him and all they had taught him. He said he was sorry to have failed them, and he assured them he would be a great engineer with God and that one day he would see them again.

"I think the world cut him off, and he was desperate," Diyer said, setting aside the papers. "Joaquin bottled all his problems up inside, he kept it all to himself. He saw the stories about families being separated on TV, and I think he was affected by that, but he never gave us any indication of what he was going to do. His goal was to get ahead, to go to school and to make something of himself, but with all the obstacles in his way he started feeling hopeless. When you're in a situation like that, you get depressed. A lot of people have told me they've thought about doing what my brother did."

Diyer and his wife, Idania, were very emotional as they talked about Joaquin. Idania, petite and pretty with a fair complexion and a gentle smile, refuses to think that Joaquin is dead. She likes to imagine that he's in another state, going to college. As she listens to Diyer describe the last time they saw Joaquin, her eyes well up with tears. It was the evening before the day he took his life, at Thanksgiving dinner. Joaquin ate turkey, played with his nieces and nephews, and installed some new programs on the computer. No one noticed anything unusual about him. But afterward, looking back, Diyer is certain that Joaquin was depressed. It was the fall of his senior year, when everyone sends applications to colleges. Even though he did apply to several colleges, his undocumented status and the very limited options for financial aid, and the fact that he could not be legally employed once he did graduate, were ever-present obstacles in his mind. But Diyer said he never talked about it. Joaquin never did anything to cause his family to worry.

On top of this bleak outlook for the future, there were other issues, like racism. Diyer does not get angry, but he's clearly exasperated as he explains that some people really don't see what's going on, but there are others who do see but do nothing. He sees it all the time when he's out on the road, when he's loading up and unloading, when he goes to a restaurant in Alabama, North Carolina, or South Carolina. Those are the people who don't want laws like the DREAM Act to ever pass, he said, even though there could be an Albert Einstein among those kids.

"Did you know that Albert Einstein wasn't born in the United States?" he said. "They don't know, and they don't know that if the DREAM Act doesn't pass, they're closing the door on someone who could do them a lot of good, someone who might cure cancer someday. If the DREAM Act had passed, my brother would still be here. His life didn't end the way it did for nothing. Only God knows why."

Then Diyer tells me about that Friday, November 25. Joaquin had gotten up early that day, as usual, to get some work done. He put his dirty laundry in the washing machine so that it would be clean for the following week. That afternoon he and his mother went over to Nina's house, and she made his favorite beef dish for dinner.

When they got home, Santa began getting ready for bed. She looked at the clock; it was 9:15 p.m. Joaquin decided to read the Bible for a bit. He chose some psalms and chapter 23 of Luke: "Truly, I say to you, today you will be with me in Paradise." A few minutes later Joaquin went to his room and changed. He put on the outfit he liked to wear for performances at church: a burgundy-colored dress shirt, black pants and jacket, and a black tie. He took the notebook with the letters to his family, his Bible, a .38-caliber pistol, and went into the bathroom. He stepped into the bathtub, placed the gun under his chin, and fired.

When Joaquin decided to take his life, he also decided that the last person he would talk to on this earth would be his brother Carlos, who lived across the street. Just minutes before firing the gun, he had called his brother on the phone to say good-bye, and to ask him to please take care of their mother. Then Joaquin hung up. Carlos knew something was wrong, and he ran across the street, asking his mother where Joaquin was. They both ran outside, thinking they would find him out back, when they heard the shot ring out. When Carlos went into the bathroom, he found his brother crumpled in the tub, his eyes half open, a faint smile on his lips, with blood gushing out of the bullet hole in his neck and chin.

Diyer got there a few minutes later. With tears running down his face, he told me how he reached for Joaquin's arm, thinking he would take him to the hospital, and just then he saw the extent of the blood loss. He picked Joaquin up as best he could, and set him down on the kitchen floor, where a large pool of blood spread. Joaquin was not breathing, he had no pulse—he was gone. Diyer thinks Joaquin had called Carlos so that his mother would not be alone when she found him.

I asked Diyer how his brother had gotten the gun.

"All kinds of things happen around here," he said. "The river is ten miles away, and Reynosa is on the other side. There's drug trafficking here and weapons trafficking. The Zetas come here. The *migra* is on every corner. And the coyotes pass through here, the smugglers. Every day on TV you see a story about how they found a thousand, two thousand pounds of drugs, they arrest them right here. It's not hard to get a gun or whatever you want. And Joaquin had his own bank account."

TANIA CHAVEZ DREAMED about one day seeing her signature printed on the one-dollar bill. For years, she admired Rosario Marin, the only person to serve as treasurer of the United States without having been born in the country. With a toothy smile, bright, shining eyes, and dark complexion, Tania had devoted most of the twenty-six years of her life to studying. First, she graduated with a degree in business administration, then she earned a master's in finance, and then she decided to go for a second master's in communications arts.

Like Joaquin, Tania was born on the Mexican side of the border, in Reynosa, and had lived in Texas since she was fourteen.

Her parents ran a small business in Reynosa, and Tania and her brother had student visas allowing them to freely come and go between there and McAllen, a common situation in border communities. The Chavez family was doing well enough—Tania's father owned a restaurant and had twelve thousand dollars in the bank, the minimum required for the United States to grant student visas for his children.

Attending school on the US side of the border meant that the constant back-and-forth gradually developed into longer and longer stays in Texas, until Tania's visits home to Mexico were sporadic and short. After a while, Tania decided to try and live with her family in Mexico. But she found that she no longer had any friends there, and the lifestyle felt strange and unfamiliar, so she soon returned to McAllen.

Things weren't easy in the United States, either. The first problem she faced was the barely masked hostility some of her teachers showed their Mexican students. When Tania was a high school sophomore, one of her teachers told her no college would accept her because her English wasn't good enough. When her classmates started talking about applying to college, Tania knew things would be twice as hard for her because she was not a permanent resident and would be ineligible for scholarships and financial aid. But she wanted to show everybody who said she'd never get into college that they were wrong. She applied to Pan Am, and a few weeks later she received their response: she had been accepted.

"I wasn't surprised," she told me, as we settled into a table at a local Starbucks. Dressed in a denim skirt, black T-shirt under a green sweater with silver stripes, and jeweled sandals, Tania has a strong, self-assured, and very feminine presence. Large jade earrings accented her lightly made-up face, framed by black hair. She set a pair of pink-framed eyeglasses down on the table before speaking.

"I came to the United States to follow my brother's dreams," she said. "I never thought it would be so hard. The first obstacle was money. I am where I am now because my parents supported me, but it's not easy paying twelve hundred dollars just to take two classes. I had to find some way to get some money. I started looking into local scholarships, and I applied for and got one that awarded me four thousand dollars for my living expenses. Those first four thousand dollars made all the difference and allowed me to keep on looking for more, because I couldn't sit around and wait for them to find me. Even now there are lots of counselors who have no idea what an undocumented student should do to be able to go to school."

Tania soon got a job as a dorm assistant at the university. Some academic institutions create positions for undocumented students who otherwise would not be able to get formal jobs. They are compensated through scholarships, meal plans, and housing, with a dorm room to live in. Through a great deal of effort, stringing together opportunities wherever she could, Tania graduated with a degree in finance in 2007. She then earned a master's in business administration.

At the time, Pan Am hosted recruiting events, inviting representatives of major corporations and organizations to come and talk to students about job and internship opportunities. Tania dreamed of one day working in the finance department of a big company like Halliburton or Procter & Gamble or even at the US Treasury Department, all of which were among those who visited Pan Am. But just as that dream seemed so tantalizingly within reach, it went up in smoke when she realized there was no way for her to change her immigration status.

"That was when it really hit me that I would not be able to get a job after I graduated. I wanted to work for one of those companies, to start a career. I wanted to have my signature on the dollar bill. I admired Rosario Marin. I talked to them, gave them my résumé, but every time—" Her voice broke. "It was a new blow for me. I had the intelligence and the talent, but I couldn't work for them. I realized that the only way I could keep going on the path I was on was to stay in school and wait for the DREAM Act to pass. That's how I started getting involved in student issues."

Added to her crushing disappointment at not being eligible to work was the recession, which also had a major impact on Mexico. The violence unleashed by President Felipe Calderon's war on the drug cartels started to affect Tania's hometown, in terms of security and economics. Her family was forced to close their restaurant. "The economy wouldn't let me realize my dreams," Tania said, as a way of explaining why she eventually gave up all hope of having a career in finance. Still, she did earn her master's degree in 2010 and then had to make a decision: go back to Mexico and start a new life in a place that no longer felt like home, or try to find some way to stay in the United States.

"My family started pressuring me: 'You're going to be twenty-five; you're not married yet. Come back to Mexico. You can get a job in a factory here. You don't have anything holding you back here. You can travel the whole world.' But my passion wasn't there," she said. "I had worked so hard and fought to start my life in the United States, and I did a good job. Why should I leave? I thought that by staying here, I wouldn't just be working for me; I could have the chance to help other students. So I made my decision, and I started working toward a second master's degree, this time in a new field, communication arts."

That decision took her life in a new direction. Over the next few years, Tania became one of the most active and visible student leaders in South Texas. In 2010, along with two others, she won Pan Am's Student Leadership Award, which recognizes students who have had a significant positive impact on student life on campus. She worked as an assistant to the dean for two years, under the same conditions as her previous job as a dorm assistant. Then the problem of her immigration status came up again: the university was going to be audited, and surely they would find out she was undocumented. Because of how the system was structured, she had been able to hold down two university jobs and, at one point, had been awarded scholarships of more than $4,500 per year. Now, in the middle of pursuing her second master's degree, she would have to move out of the dorm she had lived in for the past five years and abide by decisions made by the new administration.

It was hard to take a step backward after she had made so much progress. She managed to find a few new avenues of financial assistance and began living in her friends' dorm rooms. Because of her strong academic record and her determination, Tania was accepted to attend a seminar on leadership for Latino students, offered by Harvard University's John F. Kennedy School of Government and taught by David Gergen, a codirector of the Kennedy School's Center for Public Leadership and an adviser to four US presidents. Although the program is aimed at law students, Tania successfully pitched her case to Gergen, and she joined the group. "I found out that the 'undocumented student' identity is actually very valuable to some people in the country," she said.

After she returned from the course at Harvard, Tania had only one goal in mind: to help the student community. In October 2011 she began working on a project to advise undocumented students in McAllen high schools, creating Go Centers for undocumented students who were in their senior year, about to graduate, and unsure of how to go on to college. "I already knew how to get into college because I had done it, so I started counseling them, one at a time."

A month and a half after starting work at the Go Centers, Tania got the news that just a few miles away, in Mission, a young man in his senior year of high school had killed himself. His name was Joaquin Luna.

"That was hard," she said. "I felt so powerless, so angry. It made me so mad and so sad. I didn't know him, but since I was the only person around working with undocumented high school students, I had contact with his family. It shook me.

"What happened with Joaquin really energized the movement. We realized that in fighting for the DREAM Act, we had abandoned the students right here in the valley. But it's so hard to organize around here! Here the *migra* is on every corner, the minority is the majority, and that's why we've forgotten about our race, our people. The Latinos from here who go to college are privileged, and they feel privileged, but in the end the really privileged people in society are not going to let people from disadvantaged economic backgrounds go to college. That's a fight that we have to wage on our own."

After Joaquin's death, the Texas Dream Alliance, a state organization active in university towns like Houston and Austin, got in touch with Tania. A few days later, at a vigil held in Austin, the group's leaders publicly expressed their feeling of responsibility for Joaquin's death, once they realized their support network did not extend down to south Texas and that the students in that area were on their own. They asked Tania if she would set up a local chapter. She accepted the challenge, postponing earning her second master's degree for a few months. She began putting into practice what she had learned from her professor at Harvard, Marshall Ganz, the famed activist and organizer who had worked with Cesar Chavez back in the 1960s and whom some credited with helping in Barack Obama's victory in the 2008 presidential election, training volunteer field organizers in key states.

In April 2012 the Minority Affairs Council at Pan Am held a vigil to honor Joaquin's memory. His family attended the event, called "I Am Joaquin Luna." There were speeches calling for the passage of the DREAM Act and advocating for counseling for all students in similar circumstances. Visibly moved, Robert Nelsen, the president of Pan Am, presented Joaquin's family with his letter of acceptance, dated November 29, 2011, four days following his death.

Tania participated in the event and read an essay she had written especially for the occasion. There, in front of two hundred people, she decided to come out from the shadows and publicly acknowledge her status as an undocumented student. She said,

> There have been small steps, but we are making progress. We have been to schools in La Joya, McAllen, Edinburg, Alamo, Mission, and San Juan. We have talked with other members of the community to tell them they need to act now. In this country, of every ten Hispanics who are eligible to vote, only two do, and many of those are Republicans. The valley has its own culture. They don't believe in politics, and people say the government can't change anyway. People are disillusioned, because they see the situation in the country next door, because people who work in the fields don't have a stable income. They have to try harder, and for now that's their number one priority.

Those of us who can come and go have to get our visas renewed, hoping we don't get denied, and those of us with expired visas are trapped at the border, because to go anywhere else in the country there are immigration checkpoints. Some people have been in the area for years and have never been any farther than Laredo, a few miles away. They are confined, like on the Maria Islands [a prison in Mexico].

Joaquin Luna's death sparked outrage and interest among activist groups, but there were also negative reactions from people who opposed passage of the DREAM Act or any initiative that would benefit undocumented immigrants. While student organizations held up the case as an extreme example of the psychological and emotional pressure all Dreamers have to cope with, some comments in the media accused them of politically profiting from Joaquin's death and questioned whether his immigration status was really what motivated him to take his life, since his suicide note did not explicitly refer to the DREAM Act or his own undocumented status. In light of the controversy, Senator Dick Durbin took a large poster of Joaquin to a session of Congress and paid tribute to him on December 6, telling the boy's story and letting anyone in a similar situation know about the National Suicide Prevention Lifeline, which young people in crisis can call anytime.

Although Tania put on a brave front during our conversation, once we started talking about the future, tears of anger and frustration shone in her eyes. It was August 2012, and she was about to graduate and was once again caught in the crosshairs. Tania told me how nervous she was about possibly traveling to other states, in search of new challenges and opportunities. She talked about how her experience counseling students and helping them organize at least partly made up for her frustration and disappointment at not being able to pursue a career in her chosen field, how her failures would help her to better help others, maybe even to go to Harvard, something she had never thought she would do even in her wildest dreams. Asked what her future looks like, she said, "Well, I'd like to find a doctoral program and work in student affairs. I'd like to stay in the United States, but if that doesn't work out, I'm ready to go anyplace else in the world that appreciates what I have to offer, my experience and my intelligence. The United States was willing to pay for my two master's degrees but doesn't want to use them, so it's their loss. . . ." Tania didn't try to hold back the tears, wiping them away with her hands.

She went on, "Why can't they see they could take advantage of what I can give them and make some money? The education system figures out how to take care of us, but it can't help us once we're outside of it. My values changed in this country. I decided to make something of myself, to not get married and have children but to contribute to my community and use the education that cost me so much. My mom . . ."

Tania's voice breaks at the first mention of her mother, but she continues, "She hoped that all the years we were apart, all the birthdays and Christmases apart would be worth it in the end, and she told me that if I came back to Mexico without having resolved my situation, then all the sacrifices would have been in vain. I feel selfish. I pushed my family aside so I could go after the education I wanted. Ever since my parents' restaurant closed, they sell tacos in the plaza. How is it that they're selling tacos in the street, and I have two master's degrees and I can't help them?"

Tania is quiet for a moment. She looks at her watch and tells me she has to go. That weekend was Father's Day in Mexico, and she was going to Reynosa to be with her family. Before she leaves, she smiles and shares one more thing. "Can I tell you something? Yesterday, after Obama announced the Deferred Action program, there was a big party at Pan Am. All the students, teachers, and supporters got together. And there, I think because they were so excited, a few of them decided to come out of the shadows."

CHAPTER EIGHT

◆

DEFERRED ACTION

A Temporary Reprieve

No dream should need all this paperwork!
—Seen on a Dreamer's T-shirt

WHILE WORKING ON THIS BOOK, I became a sort of voyeur. I sat in front of my computer for hours, reading blogs, articles, and message boards hosted by Dreamer activist groups and keeping up with the latest Facebook and Twitter postings of various organizations. This Dreamer voyeurism turned into my routine.

That's how I got to know the Dreamers' day-to-day routines and how I occasionally even got involved in their lives. One day somebody shares some information about a seminar on how to apply for scholarships offered by a foundation to minority students attending college. Another day somebody else posts about a racist comment a friend of theirs had been subjected to, and others post messages of support and empathy. A young man posts about how he is selling artisan handcrafts to help pay his tuition. A professor posts a message reminding students about an upcoming deadline for applying for certain types of scholarships. An activist asks everybody to sign a petition that will be sent to a state congressional representative, urging him to enact a statewide version of the DREAM Act.

It's interesting to see how these groups, initially made up of people from the same area who already know one another, go on to expand, adding members from across the country. People from all age groups, spread out from coast to coast, who have never met face-to-face and probably never will, wind up talking to one another every day. Some become reliable sources of information. They're looking for a mentor, a counselor, or any kind of support. Sometimes I would look at the "walls" on Facebook and nothing would grab my attention from the photos posted making political jokes or the motivational messages. But on second glance, the very essence of these young people comes into focus. Sometimes somebody posts a reply to a motivational message, saying thanks because they had a horrible day or that they needed to hear it because they felt so alone. Some comments set off impassioned debates. I've seen photos or comments posted that generate more than seventy replies from other Dreamers sharing their experiences, comparing what they've been through and forming new opinions, benefiting from different perspectives. I remember one particular debate sparked by a post about checkpoints run by police on the weekends to try to catch drunk drivers. These checkpoints are also perfect tools for detaining people driving without a license, and some people complained about that in their comments. But another poster pointed out the benefit of taking drunk drivers off the road. I spent an hour looking through the replies, seeing how each person argued from their particular perspective.

I suppose anyone younger than thirty would think I'm describing something very obvious here. But for those of us who were social activists in the twentieth century and experienced assemblies and elections, street demonstrations, and long-winded debates unfolding face-to-face in cafés, virtual social organizing can be a bit hard to comprehend. It's surprising to see how people who have met only over the Internet can bond just as powerfully as if they had locked arms in a protest march.

One day, an invitation to a "summer retreat" came to me through the Facebook page of Dreams To Be Heard, an organization of Dreamers at California State University, Northridge (CSUN). According to the description, it would be a fun day in which new students could join the group and returning students could get information about the organization and "meet some sensational people."

I went to CSUN on August 3. The campus was in the heart of Northridge, in the San Fernando Valley, within the boundaries of the city of Los Angeles. An area covering about forty-four square kilometers, Northridge is known for two things. In 1994 it was proclaimed to be the epicenter of an earthquake that measured 6.7 on the Richter scale, killed sixty people, destroyed several buildings, and caused the collapse of a section of overpass on Freeway 5, the highway that runs the length of the West Coast from the US border with Mexico up to Canada. A few days after the earthquake, it was discovered that the epicenter had actually been a few blocks west, in an area of Los Angeles known as Reseda. But in the mind of the public, the deadly earthquake and Northridge would be forever intertwined.

Northridge's other claim to fame is being home to CSUN. Also known as Cal State Northridge, CSUN is one of twenty-three campuses that make up the California State University system. It was initially founded as a satellite campus of California State University, Los Angeles (CSULA), and in 1972 it took on its present name. Although it is located in a neighborhood of fewer than 50,000 residents, more than 35,000 students are enrolled at CSUN. Many students come from the local San Fernando Valley, where 42 percent of the population is Latino, a percentage point more than the 41 percent who are white.

The Dreams To Be Heard summer retreat was scheduled for the Chicano Studies Department's conference room in Jerome Richfield Hall. Many buildings and facilities on campuses throughout the California State University system bear the names of people who played an important role in the system or in the state. Dr. Richfield earned his building by founding the CSUN Philosophy Department in 1959. Today, Jerome Richfield Hall houses the College of the Humanities, which includes the Chicano Studies Department, among others.

You know you've come to the right place because the mural on the wall and almost everything else makes some allusion to the Chicano movement. The simple mural was painted to commemorate the department's thirtieth anniversary and pays homage to the leaders and cultural and ideological influences of the movement. It runs along a hallway that leads to the conference room.

I arrived at nine in the morning, just as the invitation had specified. I had been in touch with Edith, a recent graduate with a degree in graphic design who listed the three languages she spoke fluently on her Facebook profile: English, Spanish, and Spanglish. Edith had let me know that even though the invitation said the start time was at nine, it would really begin a half-hour later, so I was not surprised to see that she was the only one there. Sitting at the head of the long table that almost filled the room, Edith raised her head and looked at me unsmilingly over her glasses as I introduced myself. With a strong tone of voice, a round, serious face, and her hair pulled back tightly, Edith has everything under control. In the middle of the table she had set out the typical breakfast for students accustomed to eating on the run: water, juice, doughnuts, and bagels. A little while later another girl strode into the room and sat down at the other end of the table. It was clear they did not know each other, but after a few minutes they started talking.

Dressed in jeans and boots, with long, chestnut hair, wearing glasses and smiling brightly, the second girl introduced herself as Lorena. She said she had graduated from CSUN with a degree in psychology and now was earning her master's in education at New Mexico State University. Lorena had been one of the founding members of Dreams To Be Heard in 2007. She had been in Los Angeles when she heard about this meeting and decided to come and find out what was happening. I found out later she had also attended because she was doing a school project on undocumented immigrants, and during one of the breaks she asked people to fill out a questionnaire, which would be a part of her research.

While Lorena and Edith talked about the group and how it had evolved, I heard several terms that would be used frequently during the meeting. Those who were not undocumented described themselves as "allies," since being sympathetic to the cause is not the same as actually living the life of a Dreamer, day in and day out.

"I have never been undocumented, but some people in my family are," said Lorena. "I know being documented is a privilege. I know because I saw my friends, I see every day how hard it is to go to school if you're undocumented, so that's why I joined the group."

Edith nods approvingly. The others start coming in while she talks about how other similar groups have formed and grown. Partly for the benefit of the people just arriving, Edith mentions how a worry many of them share is being exposed. Lorena replies in English, but when she talks about trust, the word comes out in Spanish: "You have to create an environment that makes you feel safe, *que te de confianza.*"

At one point Edith looks Lorena in the eye, very serious. "What you did is really important," she tells her. "I've heard about the ones who started the group, but I hadn't met any."

A little after ten, there was a quorum to start the meeting. Everyone took a seat around the long table, surrounded by bookcases that reached almost all the way to the ceiling, filled with books on Mexican and Latin American history, the history of the United States, labor relations, social struggles, contemporary literature, and, of course, Chicano culture. Everyone listened intently around the table that day, as the group discussed the chapter in history they had been invited to write.

ALTHOUGH MANY ORGANIZED groups of Dreamers experienced a swell in membership in 2007 after the DREAM Act failed to pass, coordinated student efforts had begun a few years before that, with the surge of an organization known as IDEAS. In October 2003, with the support of university faculty and administrators, some UCLA students created Improving Dreams, Equality, Access, and Success with the aim of motivating and inspiring other students to go on to college after graduating from high school, providing financial aid, guidance, support, and access to other resources. The group's founders focused their initial efforts on educating the community about AB 540, a state law enacted in 2001 that allowed undocumented students who met certain requirements to pay in-state tuition rates.

Over the following months, other, smaller groups began forming. One of them was Dreams To Be Heard, which began meeting informally in 2006 and 2007, and had the same goal of supporting students who could benefit from AB 540. Since then, the group has included dozens of students and has connected with the larger network of Dreamer organizations. For the most part, these smaller, local groups do an amazing job of conserving their autonomy and meeting the specific needs of their members, while also supporting and being sustained by the larger national network. The strength of one to give strength to all, and vice versa.

"Even when we're a dysfunctional family, we're still a family because we've had this experience of being undocumented, and we understand."

Edith opened the meeting with this affirmation, which I will realize a few days later has made a deep impression on those in the group. The reference to a family formed around a common struggle will appear again and again in exchanges on the group's Facebook page. Seated around a table, the members of this new family, who mostly speak English with some Spanish mixed in here and there, introduced themselves. Adriana, a slender, energetic girl majoring in urban planning, greeted everyone in the room warmly when she came in, including me. Gabriela, petite with dark hair, studies political science. Jesus, studying sociology and medicine, was born in the United States but joined IDEAS as a high school student "because I knew people who were undocumented, but I didn't really understand all the challenges they face every day."

The day's session began as these types of meetings and seminars typically do when the participants don't know each other, with a group exercise meant to help break the ice. They played a word game in which the first person would say the name of an animal, and the next person would name an animal that began with the last letter of the previous animal and so on: dog, goat, turtle, elephant. After a little while, the game changed to naming countries or states, and then foods. So as they made their way through *cat, Missouri,* and *hot cakes,* they revealed much about themselves and where they came from, and how the cultures of two countries had indelibly marked them, affecting how they thought, their memories, their favorite foods, and their daily experiences.

"Okay, now let's do foods," Edith said and started by naming chicken. The others followed, naming things they typically ate, like meat, avocados, corn, sushi, nachos, and teriyaki. After a while, without even thinking about it, they switched into Spanish, as they did so many times every day: *espinacas, salchichas, rábanos, esquites, enchiladas,* and *salsa* are some of the foods they mentioned. As it went on, the game seemed to represent a kind of inventory of Los Angeles cuisine, its culture, and the reality of these young people and an entire community, a reality that some still refuse to acknowledge.

ON JUNE 14, 2012, *Time* published one of its most controversial covers in recent years. The cover photo shows young people of various races and ethnicities, none of them white, against a dark background, as if they were emerging from the shadows. They stare directly into the camera with serious expressions. The tag line across the photo reads, "We Are Americans," and below that, in smaller type and next to an asterisk, it says, "Just not legally." Although the story would run in its June 25 issue, the magazine's editors decided to release the cover photo two weeks before that. Questions about what motivated the image's early release became secondary once the media firestorm began over the photo, which depicts thirty-six young undocumented immigrants publicly announcing their status on the cover of one of the most widely read magazines in the world, while also claiming to be just as American as anybody who had been born in the United States.

The cover story had been written by Jose Antonio Vargas, a thirty-one-year-old journalist and, now, activist originally from the Philippines who had been sent to live with his grandparents in California when he was twelve. Jose Antonio discovered he was undocumented when he applied for a driver's license using his green card, and it was found to be fraudulent. In spite of this, Vargas attended and graduated from college, became a journalist, and in 2008 was part of the team of *Washington Post* reporters to win a Pulitzer Prize for reporting on the Virginia Tech massacre, in which thirty-two people were shot dead and seventeen others were wounded by a South Korean student.

In 2011 Vargas published an article about the most moving story he had ever witnessed: his own. "My Life as an Undocumented Immigrant" ran in the *New York Sunday Times* on June 22 and caused an uproar. A year later, Vargas outed himself again, on the cover of *Time*.

Less than twenty-four hours after the *Time* cover was publicized, the reason for its early release became clear. The following day, President Obama officially announced the launch of the Deferred Action program for young undocumented immigrants. The story was breaking news in US media and was even covered outside of the United States. The Dreamers were the topic of conversation across the country, and they began to see a faint light at the end of a tunnel that had been dark for so long.

The announcement of the Deferred Action for Childhood Arrivals program, or DACA, as it came to be known, represented a small victory for Dreamers across the nation. The potential beneficiaries, who could number 1.6 million adults under the age of thirty-one, according to conservative estimates, or as many as 2.1 million, according to more recent studies, could obtain a work permit and a valid Social Security number for two years, in the hope that when the two years were up it could be renewed or that the DREAM Act would have passed by then. But DACA is just a temporary administrative version of the DREAM Act, its announcement strategically timed to best support Barack Obama's reelection campaign; it does not grant permanent legal status or provide any pathway to citizenship. Of course, those who could benefit were thrilled at the prospect of getting a Social Security number, permission to work, fair wages, and eligibility to receive social services in their communities. Some applied for the program immediately—if they could afford the $400 application fee—and by October their documentation began to arrive.

But after the initial euphoria began to wear off, a question arose that they talked about quietly among themselves, then more openly on websites and Internet forums, and a few months later they began directly asking officials and politicians: what was going to happen if Obama lost the election? What if the Republican presidential nominee, Mitt Romney, who had publicly declared his opposition to the DREAM Act and favored promoting "self-deportation" as an immigration policy, became the next president? The Dreamers were aware that by applying for the Deferred Action program, they were officially acknowledging their undocumented status to federal immigration authorities. Clinging to a ray of hope, they were going "all in," and betting it all.

EDITH LED THE DISCUSSION on the most important topic: politics. The group started talking about problems that might not have seemed entirely relevant to non-students but are of extreme importance to students dependent on certain kinds of aid. For example, the recently passed California DREAM Act had just gone into effect, and some in attendance knew people who had submitted applications for state financial aid programs and had been rejected for no apparent reason. It seemed to be a common complaint. Some of those who were attending a meeting for the first time watched and listened as more-experienced students spoke up. The boldest among them ranted about university administrators.

"You have to stay right on top of them so they do their jobs. For three years there have been budget cuts, so they're not going to go around looking for you to give you money," said one of the young women emphatically.

Another explained that just by putting a little pressure on administrative staff, they will respond and do something. "If you don't," she said, "you're the one who will suffer the consequences. You have to go to the university president or the dean and tell them about what is going on in the financial aid department. If we don't bring it up with them, this is just going to keep happening."

Iris, one of the most outspoken in the group, asserted that as far as the university was concerned, the students were just a way for them to make money. Lorena was surprised by how widespread the problem was and offered to give advice to students on Facebook. Edith mentioned that she knew students at other schools who were having the same issues. Ricardo pointed out that as far as scholarships went, a number was assigned to each application, whether the applicant was documented or not. So in theory at least, a student's undocumented status did not factor into a decision to reject his or her application.

While some students talked, the others around the table took notes, doodled, or looked at their phones. Rarely did they actually look at the speaker the whole time they spoke. Two students surfed the Web on their laptops, looking things up on Google as the discussion unfolded. No one seemed offended by all the multitasking. As they tried to come up with a strategy to open up greater access to scholarship funds, I looked around the room. The walls were covered with photos, posters, and artwork depicting the Chicano struggle and culture. I saw a poster with two students studying, superimposed over a picture of a pair of Mexican folkloric dancers, with the seal of the Mexican flag and an Aztec calendar. All the imagery from the motherland was a bit overwhelming. A poster in an angular style reminiscent of Soviet constructivism depicted a couple of students looking off toward the horizon. Its tag line read, "Our dream can't wait." Next to it hung a black-and-white photo of some children holding up a sign marking 3000 Brooklyn Place in East Los Angeles. That sign was taken down and replaced by another in 1994, when that part of the street was renamed for Cesar Chavez. Today, on the corner of East Cesar E. Chavez and North Evergreen avenues is a mural honoring members of the United Farm Workers of America.

When it was time to turn the discussion to DACA, Edith sat back and let another young woman take the lead. Rosa, a pretty, fair-skinned girl with a round face, curly hair, and glasses, had been researching on the Internet since the beginning of the meeting and shared what she found with the group. She worked for CHIRLA (Coalition for Humane Immigrant Rights of Los Angeles), the organization that just a few weeks before had honored State Assemblyman Gil Cedillo, and her job was to maintain the momentum of their voter-registration campaign leading up to the November 2012 elections. She smiled warmly and gestured with her hands as she talked about how she wants President Obama to be reelected. Even though he hasn't turned out to be everything we wanted, Rosa told the group, for now he's the best option we have.

One issue relating to DACA took on particular importance: how the general public perceives the difference, if any, between that program and the DREAM Act. Rosa and some others expressed concern that the public may think the president was announcing that the DREAM Act had been passed. Apparently it was a common misperception, as hundreds of messages were posted on social media during that time to congratulate the president or question him for supposedly passing the DREAM Act, something that could have happened only if Congress had brought it up for a vote. This naturally brought the discussion around to Obama and the upcoming election, since it was clear to everyone that the Dreamers had become a political tool for the White House.

"Maybe we haven't seen all the change that we would have wanted," said Edith, taking the lead again with her strong, clear voice, her expression serious, "but we are making progress. Remember what happened with the California DREAM Act? It was vetoed twice before a new administration came into power, and then it had a real chance. Things could be better with Obama in his second term, and DACA is a good sign."

Before breaking for lunch, the group did another team-building exercise. We all went outside. When Edith gave the signal, we had to quickly form groups composed of whatever number she said: three, five, or two people. Then, as a group, we had to hug. Everyone rushed around, quickly drawn together and clinging to one another, then formed new combinations, with people who had been total strangers just a few hours before locking in warm embraces. The exercise ended and two students arrived with lunch, burritos and nachos for everybody.

On August 3, Gabriela posted a photo from the summer retreat:

A family like none other <3.

Edith posted on August 8:

Please, help one of our members. She's looking for a place to live near CSUN as soon as possible and can pay up to $300 (if possible), she'll take any available space (living room, bedroom . . .) If any of you or anybody you know needs a roommate, please post a reply here. Thanks in advance.

Michie posted on August 24:

WARNING! There will be several check points starting tomorrow around NoHo and Van Nuys. Read this link to find out more and pass it on! :D

Lucia posted on August 24:

Beautiful dreamers, do any of you know of any free or low-cost health services for undocumented adults? I have a client in urgent need of hospitalization, but he has not done it because of the cost. He has symptoms of high blood pressure and could be suffering a heart attack and is experiencing a lot of pain. I want to enroll him in some program that could at least absorb some of the costs. Please let me know if you know about anything.

On September 12, Adriana posted about a reading list on urban planning:

Does anybody know somebody who could lend or sell me these books at a good price? Any help would be much appreciated, please let me know as soon as you can. I need to catch up on lectures and assignments by next week at the latest. Thanks in advance!

Rosa posted on September 13:

> Hi, today and tomorrow we need volunteers at CHIRLA between
> 10 AM and 6 PM to help us prepare for the launch of our
> Election Campaign this Saturday. We would really appreciate
> any help you could give.

Yesica posted on September 19:

> The Latino journalism students at CSUN are having a bake sale
> in front of Manzanita Hall from 11 until 2 PM. Come by for
> some yummy treats

On September 27, Maritza posted a photo of a design for a T-shirt:

> I'm making T-shirts for the Dream Team! Half of the funds
> raised will go to a lucky dreamer so they can start their
> DACA application!

Gabriela posted on October 3:

> I got my work permit ;) What's next? Fighting for my friends and
> my parents!

On October 23, Edith posted a photo of herself, her usually serious expression replaced by an ecstatic smile as she held her Social Security card up for the camera:

> IT'S HERE!!!!!!! :D What's been missing for twenty years of
> my life

> For all of you who were born here or who became legal
> residents or citizens, never forget what a privilege it is to have
> this card. Now I have to go to work $$

CHAPTER NINE

---◆---

UNDOCUQUEERS

Coming Out, Twice

*Why is it that, as a culture,
we are more comfortable seeing two men
holding guns than holding hands?*

—ERNEST J. GAINES

IN THE DARKNESS, a spotlight shines on one end of a backyard, an improvised stage of sorts next to a little platform where a DJ plays music. The Mexican pop star Gloria Trevi's voice pumps through the speakers, belting out a song about beautiful women who rebel against convention, discover their strength, and take on the world. The chatter of conversations rippling through the crowd suddenly goes quiet, and then everyone erupts in one jubilant roar. The spotlight settles on a figure in a red fishnet dress and a black bra, with boyshorts hugging firm, narrow hips and silky smooth brown skin clearly outlined underneath. Black stockings, sparkling platform shoes, and a long black wig complete the striking look. Swaying her hips, trying not to wobble atop her dramatically high heels, she takes a step forward, and then another; she turns her head and offers the crowd a sultry look. They quiet down expectantly, and Maria sin Papeles (Maria with No Papers) takes charge.

Maria's small, almond-shaped eyes seem to twinkle ironically as a mysterious smile plays on her lips. Her thick, darkly lined eyebrows arch over long false eyelashes. It's surprising to see this new face and personality that Maria brings to Jorge's life. Because when she scrubs off the makeup, peels away the false eyelashes, takes off

159

her high heels, dress, bra, and stockings and tucks the wig away in a drawer to reveal an almost-shaved head, it's Jorge's warm, honest gaze and his calm, quiet expression that dominates.

JUST AS WITH EVERY DREAMER I MEET, I found out about Jorge through someone else, who had met him through a friend. I met him in El Hormiguero, a community center in the San Fernando Valley in northern Los Angeles, where students, activists, and other members of the community hold meetings on various topics. The meeting where I met Jorge had such a provocative title, I had no choice but to go and see what it was all about: "Undocuqueer Healing Oasis." It was a space where gays, lesbians, bisexuals, transvestites, and transgender people could share their experiences and talk about what it's like to live with not just one but two identities that go against the accepted norm. They share how they struggle to get ahead or just keep going, even though it takes more work, and sometimes you just feel tired and overwhelmed.

Jorge was the special guest at this session. The meetings at El Hormiguero usually have ten to fifteen participants, sometimes more. At each one, someone is invited to share an experience in a particular area that he or she has to deal with every day or to tell a success story. Jorge's area of struggle is definitely coming to terms with his identity as an "undocuqueer."

Jorge was born in El Cora, a ranching area in the state of Nayarit, Mexico. His family was poor and made their living by farming. His father grew papayas, mangos, cocoa, and avocados to feed the family and to sell. As the children got older, they helped out with the crops.

Jorge's parents' relationship was far from perfect. His childhood was scarred by domestic violence and abuse. Even now, at twenty-eight, looking back on what he calls "my first confrontation with injustice" caused his voice to break with emotion. When he was six or seven, he already knew he was different by the way he played with the other children and how he felt, but at the time he didn't understand exactly what it was. And he knew his parents noticed too, but they never talked about it with him. One day Jorge was playing with a little girl, and although he doesn't remember the exact nature of the game, he remembers very well that it was something that irritated his father to no end when he came home from work and saw them. His father grabbed Jorge by his shirt and violently yanked him up, then threw him onto the floor and said, "I don't want any faggots in my house."

"I didn't cry. I was more confused than angry, because I didn't know what he was calling me, but I could tell by his tone of voice and how he was treating me that it was something really bad," Jorge said, his eyes wide, as if he were remembering something that had happened just a few days ago. "Ever since then, I knew I was different."

For Jorge, his journey across the border was a pleasant, almost happy experience. He remembers a little pickup truck with almost ten people riding in the back that left from Tepic, the capital of Nayarit, and drove up to Tijuana. They got there on a Friday around noon and crossed the border later that day when an uncle came to pick them up. By eight o'clock that evening they were in their new home. Since his uncle was documented and had a car, they had worked it out to cross over with him (Jorge reminded me that the situation at the border was very different sixteen years ago, in a pre-9/11 world). An aunt was waiting for them, and so began Jorge's new life in Orange County, about forty miles south of Los Angeles. Unlike other Dreamers who describe their arrival in the United States as marking a painful rupture with their previous life in Mexico, Jorge recalled it as a positive time. Although it marked the beginning of his life as an undocumented immigrant, it also put an end to his father's physical and emotional abuse.

While his mother worked cleaning houses, her children started going to school. It was hardest for her oldest son, as adapting to a new culture and language at eighteen was not easy. It was easier for Jorge and his other brother, who was one year younger. They were able to make friends and always attended the same school. Even though everything was going pretty well, Jorge always felt burdened by the stigma of being "different." Now he knew that there were other people like him, and he had the words to identify himself. He knew he was gay, but he could not say it openly.

"At that age, thirteen, fourteen years old, I liked one boy and then another," Jorge said. "Your body is changing, but I couldn't enjoy those experiences because I had the shadow of my father hanging over me. At the time I wanted to tell my mom, but I was afraid she would react the same way my father did. What had happened with him kept me from coming out of the closet; it haunted me. Those were at least two very dark years in my life. I was depressed and had low self-esteem; it was really painful. I felt like my mom could tell, but she didn't have the vocabulary to ask me."

Until one day she did find the words. As they were driving home one afternoon, Jorge's mother stopped the car at a red light, turned down the radio, looked over at her son, and said in her gentlest tone of voice, "I want to ask you something because I'm confused: Do you like boys or girls?"

Jorge thought of his father and felt the pain rising in him as strongly as ever as he turned away. His first impulse was to lie and say he liked girls, to protect himself.

"I like boys."

The light changed, and his mother kept driving. She pulled the car into a parking lot, turned off the engine, and got out. Jorge imagined the worst: she was leaving him there alone in the middle of the parking lot, in his school uniform. Alone. In spite of his panic, a strange feeling of relief washed over him for a fraction of a second, knowing that he had told the truth. But then something entirely unexpected happened: his mother opened his car door and gave him a hug: "Maybe I don't understand what's happening," she said, "but we'll figure it out together. We'll be okay."

Now the emotion that Jorge hadn't conveyed as he told me about his immigration experience broke through the surface as he remembered that special moment.

"A woman on her own, an undocumented immigrant, who only went to school until the second grade, challenging the system, fighting machismo, and homophobia, and relying on her love for me as a mother—she said: This is my son, and I'm going to protect him. In that moment all the pain that my father caused started to melt away, little by little, and I started to enjoy being gay. I told some of my friends, even some teachers at school, and I began to feel supported and loved," he said.

"I knew that my father had renounced our relationship. I've tried to reconcile with him, but he didn't care . . . I recently made the decision to not let him have that power over me. For two years, I've had to work with that pain and tell myself that it was time to let the wound heal, what happened wasn't my fault. I've tried to understand where my father was coming from, a Catholic, *machista* family. In a way he is a victim of those belief systems, and if he decided to close the door, that's on him. I have to be happy and heal the pain so I can experience intense love and happiness and not let that scar me."

Though Jorge took an important step forward by accepting his homosexual identity, there was another bitter pill left to swallow with his immigration status. Thanks to their mother's strength and determination the Gutierrez children had enjoyed a certain degree of stability by living in the same neighborhood. But when it came time to go off to college, it was the same old story: the crushing implications of being undocumented hit them head-on.

"You start to see what being undocumented means, but you don't really get it until your friends from school start getting driver's licenses and you can't, and that's really hard," Jorge said. "You want to get a job, but you don't have a Social Security number, and when you fill in your college application and it asks you for that number again, and you know you don't have one . . . I felt like that was somehow going to magically change. I came home and asked my mom, 'Do I have a Social Security number?' And I already knew the answer, but I felt like something was going to change during the walk home from school."

I stopped Jorge at this point in his story. As I was writing this book, many Dreamers expressed to me that same hope that something magical would somehow occur to change their circumstances. I remembered Catalina, the girl from Alabama who had tearfully told me about her high school graduation, as she had fervently waited for her name to be called from the list of students who were going on to college, even though she had not even filled out an application. I asked Jorge what he thought was behind this.

"I think when you get here as a child and they tell you if you get good grades, if you're a good student, you can be whatever you want," Jorge said. "So you think things are going to change, that you're special, and that's not going to happen to you. But life is different. At the time I sent my application to California State University, Fullerton, based on a counselor's advice. It was a very difficult experience for me. I was really mad at my family, at my situation, for not having any resources, for not being able to go to the school I wanted, because I really wanted to go to Berkeley."

The first three years at Fullerton were utterly exhausting for Jorge. His mother kept on working to support the family, but she had no money to help with school, so Jorge had been working since he was fourteen. While he went to college, he worked at a pizzeria, an ice cream parlor, and a photo store and helped his mother on weekends with a side business doing party decorations. The money he earned went toward tuition, clothes, books, and sometimes helping with the rent. Jorge went from home to work and back again. He felt frustrated and questioned whether what he was doing made any sense. He didn't know how to talk about it, and he didn't know anybody in the same situation he was in. Then, a semester before graduation, just as he was about to throw in the towel, he was invited to join the Orange County Dream Team.

MAY 17, 2005, holds a special place in the hearts of Latinos in Los Angeles. On that day, Antonio Villaraigosa was elected the first mayor of Mexican origin since 1872. Six weeks later, on July 1, the swearing-in ceremony was held on the southern staircase of the beautiful City Hall building, which had been inspired by the Grecian Mausoleum at Halicarnassus. Stone from each of California's fifty-eight counties and water from its twenty-one historical missions had been used to form the building's concrete. In his speech that day, Villaraigosa talked about unity, saying that as he walked through the building's doors, he would not be alone: he stood on the shoulders of those who had come before him and had fought for Hispanics to be represented in government, paving the way for generations to come.

Seven years later, a few blocks from City Hall in Pershing Square, a small park surrounded by corporate office buildings and luxury hotels, a group of student activists once again made May 17 a day to remember. Just like on the earlier May 17, words like "United States," "justice," "future," and "opportunity" were said in the speeches protesters gave. Only this time they were not celebrating a victory but demanding a fundamental right: the Dreamers' right to keep on dreaming.

The Right to Dream campaign had been launched nationally by United We Dream in early 2012. Its objective was to organize the hundreds of groups that their network comprises in cities, counties, and states across the country, and carry out a coordinated action demanding that the federal government immediately stop deporting students. Through specific actions, they tried to convey the harsh reality in which undocumented students must live. They called for the right to travel freely, allowing a teen to take his little sister to school without being afraid of getting arrested; the right to meaningfully contribute to their communities, allowing a young woman to use her law degree to get a well-paying job; the right to live with their loved ones, which is shattered every time someone gets deported; the right to dream, something that has been denied to Dreamers for more than twelve years. The action would begin all across the country at ten in the morning, Los Angeles time, on May 17, 2012.

Dozens of young people wearing T-shirts emblazoned with the word "Undocumented" and featuring images referencing the Dream Act—such as the traffic sign picturing Dreamers crossing the street that I had seen in Gil Cedillo's office—gathered in the park that morning and began their protest. Several speakers shared their experience of being undocumented, acknowledging their immigration status out loud, proclaiming they were not afraid. Many of them called Barack Obama's deportation policies into question, urging him to make some concessions before asking for the Latino community's vote the following November. Later, they crossed the street and headed toward the building housing the federal immigration courts, demanding that they be allowed to go in and talk to the authorities directly. Of course, that did not happen. So they marched in front of the building in a circle, holding up signs explaining the difference between a Dreamer and a criminal, with the slogan "Obama, you can't court us and deport us," while a homeless man applauded them, and office workers from surrounding buildings looked out their windows, coffee and sandwiches in hand, watching the unusual protest unfolding before them on a Thursday at lunchtime.

While most of the protesters carried their signs and shouted slogans, I struck up a conversation with a young man named Luis, who was a member of the San Fernando Valley Dream team, and he told me about his own right to dream. "It's not fair that we don't have the same rights as other couples to get an interview with immigration, like people who marry a US citizen of the opposite sex." Then he told me he was an "undocuqueer" and was in a group, and he invited me to come to one of their meetings at El Hormiguero in the San Fernando Valley.

WHEN I WAS A TEENAGER, I read a rather obscure book, a first novel by an unknown writer, Chuck Barris. Twenty years later I found out that he wasn't as unknown as I had thought, first because he was a successful game-show producer in the United States— the short novel he had written was semi-autobiographical—and second, because he went on to write *Confessions of a Dangerous Mind*, an autobiography about his life allegedly as a CIA agent that was adapted into a movie starring George Clooney. But in Barris's novel, there's a scene in which a man asks someone what he thought of California after visiting. The person replies that it was as if someone had grabbed the whole country by one end and shaken it, and everything that was loose had settled in California.

That vibrant description had stayed with me subconsciously for many years and gradually rose to the surface of my mind when I arrived in Los Angeles. In effect, everything seemed to have found a place there: the glamour of Hollywood; the African American struggle for civil rights; the heart of Chicano culture; billions of dollars' worth of imports that arrived from Asia through the Los Angeles port; an inefficient public transportation system; low-rider cars; and the best Thai food in the world—some claim it's even better than in Thailand. But out of all the areas of Los Angeles, if I had to pick just one that best embodied Barris's description, it would be the San Fernando Valley.

Maybe there are many cities in the world like this, but when I came to Los Angeles, to me it was a novelty: the city is bisected by a little mountain range, the Santa Monica Mountains, like a scar dividing Los Angeles almost in half. The area to the south of the mountains, known as the Basin, is flanked by the ocean on two sides, with beaches on one side and the port on the other. Central Los Angeles, including the city's downtown, Hollywood, and Boyle Heights, is in the Basin. To the north of the mountains lies the San Fernando Valley, with another range, the Santa Susana Mountains, running along its northernmost reaches. Between these two mountainous borders, the Valley is home to 1.7 million of Los Angeles' 3.7 million inhabitants.

Although in the past, several aerospace companies and nuclear research facilities were located there, since the 1970s the Valley has also been home to major Hollywood movie studios. The iconic Hollywood sign overlooking the neighborhood of the same name sits atop the south side of the mountains, prompting Los Angelinos who live in the Basin to say that residents of the Valley live "on the wrong side of the hill." But now CBS, NBC, ABC, Universal Studios, Nickelodeon, the Walt Disney Company, and Warner Brothers also reside on "the wrong side."

Aside from the glamorous movie studios, the Valley is home to another powerful sector of the entertainment world, somewhat less glitzy but just as successful: the porn industry. In the 1970s, as the large and midsized postproduction companies and businesses renting film equipment moved into the area, pioneers of the pornographic movie industry followed—and flourished—generating $13.3 billion in 2006 alone. Although with the Internet boom it is difficult to come up with completely accurate figures, analysts of the industry often say that nine out of ten pornographic movies or videos in the United States are filmed or produced in the San Fernando Valley.

The combination of all of these factors may have given rise in the 1980s to the "Valley Girl," a stereotypical young, middle- or upper-middle-class white woman benefiting from a booming economy, possibly with ties to the Hollywood movie machine. These women were arrogant, very materialistic, and shallow, much more concerned about their social status and physical appearance than with their personal or intellectual development. Although you can still see this type at shopping malls, restaurants, and gyms in neighborhoods like Studio City and Toluca Lake, over the past decade or so a new breed of hipsters have made their presence felt: they ride bikes, buy organic food, are interested in art, and generally tend to vote Democrat.

Despite the recent demographic changes that have affected Los Angeles and the Valley, the rise in the number of Hispanics being the most dramatic, the area still has a sizeable white population. Whites make up a larger percentage of the overall population in the Valley, at 41 percent of the total, than in the basin, where they represent 28 percent of residents. Latinos make up 42 percent of the population in the Valley, less than the 48 percent of Latinos in Los Angeles as a whole. Only 4 percent of Valley residents are African American, while they make up 11 percent of the total population of Los Angeles. Although there are other ethnic and cultural groups with a strong presence, such as the Armenian community, the Valley is basically evenly divided between whites and Latinos.

Most of the Latinos living in the area are immigrants or children of immigrants, and though for obvious reasons there are no exact numbers for the undocumented population, they are a significant presence. This is clear from noticing all the small businesses offering check-cashing services without requiring identification and wiring money to Mexico and Central America. There are also businesses offering credit to anyone, regardless of their lack of credit history; lawyers specializing in representing workers who have experienced abuse in the workplace because of their undocumented status; and immigration lawyers. And the undocumented community experiences a kind of mass panic when checkpoints are set up to catch drunk drivers and police demand to see driver's licenses. Although many people living in the Valley have been there for years because of their work in the movie industry or related businesses—postproduction, costume rental, set construction, catering, transportation—for some families, the Valley is basically a dormitory, and they work on the other side of the mountains, in the Basin or in other towns in Los Angeles County. Many of them have come to the valley to improve their quality of life, moving from areas like South Central LA, where the rent may be cheaper but the crime rates and levels of gang activity are higher. Still, some neighborhoods in the Valley have household incomes that are right around the poverty line.

Walking around, one may see a little of everything, coexisting in a state of calculated chaos—as if someone had grabbed the whole country by one end and shaken it, and everything that was loose had landed in the San Fernando Valley.

THE FIRST TIME I VISITED THE HORMIGUERO, I had a hard time finding it. The group's founders had chosen as their headquarters a house in Pacoima, a neighborhood along the northern edge of the Valley, very close to the Santa Susana Mountains. The land begins to rise there, and the streets are like little mountain ranges themselves, snaking up and down the hillsides, lined by nicely kept houses, many with visible clues about their inhabitants' origins, like a Virgin of Guadalupe on display near the front door. Half of the residents of Pacoima are immigrants, and seven in ten are Mexican or of Mexican descent.

The Hormiguero is a community space that from the outside looks like a regular house, with a lovely little garden out front. The front steps lead up to a double wooden door, and inside the entry-way a large poster greets visitors, reading:

The Hormiguero is a safe space
No racism
No sexism
No ageism
No ableism
No homophobia
No transphobia
No xenophobia
Please check your privilege at the door

The interior of the house is really interesting. It's split-level, conforming to the terrain it was built on, and has the feel of a home that was once occupied by an average family and gradually transitioned to the communal space it is now. The furnishings and decorative touches tell the story. The living room has finely uphol-stered, oversized armchairs positioned around a huge coffee table of highly polished dark wood. A dining room table made of iron, although of high quality, clashes somewhat with the room, and an elegant chandelier overhead contrasts sharply with decorations of a more ideological bent: a picture of a Native American cradling a shotgun, saying, "Show me your papers" and a poster of Che Guevara. Hand-woven blankets and serapes from Latin America are draped over the armchairs. A tapestry hung on the wall reads, "*Viva los trabajos colectivos. Viva el EZLN*," alongside bookcases stuffed with books. Pots hold little aloe plants, and leaflets and flyers hang from a string stretched across the wall, as if they were clothes hung out to dry. On the lower level, in the garage, there's an area for bicycle repair. Next to the dining room, a glass door leads out to a terrace with a garden. The highest level has bedrooms, the only part of the house with any real privacy.

Marcos Zamora-Sanchez is one of El Hormiguero's founders. With dark skin, longish hair and a little scruffy-looking with a beard and wearing big glasses, he explains the evolution of the space as fulfilling a personal need to be in tune with his community. As an activist involved with cultivating leadership in various human rights organizations and with the University of Southern California, one of the most expensive and prestigious universities in the area, he is accustomed to giving talks and participating in debates and seminars on immigration but always in academic environments. One day, he realized that all of that work, confined exclusively to academic settings, was never going to reach the community. So he decided to take his work outside of that environment and bring it to the heart of Pacoima. Marcos and the six others who now live in the house have an understanding that their doors are open to whoever needs to be there, whether they need to borrow a book, use the Internet, hold meetings, screen movies, hold workshops, or even throw a party.

One of the first organizations to make use of the space was the San Fernando Valley Dream Team (SFVDT). When I met Luis at the demonstration in Pershing Square, we talked for a while about his undocuqueer identity and his organizing work in the Dreamer movement. He ended up inviting me to come to a meeting, which brought me to the Hormiguero.

On the evening of the SFVDT meeting, I arrived at the house in Pacoima at seven o'clock sharp and found four guys in the living room, lounging on the overstuffed armchairs covered in serapes. There were bags of chips, Bimbo bread, and soft drinks set out on the coffee table and a bottle of Jarritos, a Mexican soda, on the dining room table.

Along with Luis, there were Ernesto, Adrian, and Agustin. Ernesto was Luis's boyfriend, and it was clear that they have all known one another for a while and feel very comfortable together and right at home in that space. They each had their laptops open, and once the meeting officially began, they got started. This semester, the group had ten members, and their bylaws state that they can have a quorum with a minimum of four members present.

That meeting's agenda included updates on legislation relating to the DREAM Act, on the federal and state level; updates on their social media platforms, including adding photos from the Pershing Square event to their website and Facebook page; providing assistance to people who needed help filling out college applications; an initiative to create and sell T-shirts with the organization's logo; and holding a movie night fund-raiser, which they'll have to talk to their city councilman, Richard Alarcon, about regarding a space to hold the event. I am surprised by how comfortable they are talking about approaching authority figures.

The tone of the discussion was light and pleasant. As I have seen with other Dreamer groups, everybody was on their computers as they talked; it was clear that to everybody under thirty, giving anyone 100 percent of their attention was a waste of time. As they ran down the agenda, some announcements were made: the next day, there would be a roadblock at a nearby intersection to catch drunk drivers, and they would need to send out an alert to the community. A sister organization in San Francisco had sent them an invitation, and they needed to see whether they could make the trip and how many could go. Agustin announced that he was going to receive a prize for a photograph he entered in a contest. The title of the photo was *The Dream Is Coming*.

Luis, age twenty-four, led the meeting. Tall and lanky, with fair skin, black hair, and small, smiling eyes, he was friendly and pleasant but firm when he needed to get the group to focus on their agenda. He majored in Chicano studies at UCLA. The pride he felt when he openly described himself as an "undocuqueer" was obvious. "Now, I know it's not fair for you to have to live your life always hiding, ashamed," he said. "I went through a time like that, until I came out as queer at twenty-one. Coming out as undocumented took me a little longer."

Luis and his family came to the United States from Zacatecas, Mexico, when he was four. He is the second of six children, three born in the United States and three in Mexico. He has lived almost his whole life in the San Fernando Valley, which he describes as a safe environment for undocumented immigrants. Because so many of the residents there are in the same circumstances, there are support networks, unwritten laws, and unspoken understandings even with authority figures, who generally let people go about their lives without interfering. Maintaining that veneer of calm normalcy depends on everyone following several unwritten rules. Among those rules, Jorge learned to live with two: never mention your immigration status and never talk about your sexual orientation.

Ever since he was thirteen, Luis knew he wanted to go to UCLA. As a resident of the San Fernando Valley, he won scholarships to attend Valley College, where he spent two years studying psychology. From there he applied to transfer to UCLA to finish his degree and was accepted. The day he got the news of his acceptance, Luis said he felt like "I was handed the key to go where I'd always wanted, but I didn't have the money."

He decided to enroll anyway and somehow figure out a way to pay for it. He managed to get through the first quarter relying on his savings, and he immediately started working at a Jack in the Box restaurant to earn some money for the next one. But then he had to take a break from school because he couldn't afford a third quarter right away. He went to work full time, saved as much as he could, and was able to reenroll two quarters later.

The key that was handed to Luis with his acceptance to UCLA not only opened the doors of higher education he had always dreamed about. It also opened up two others: the doors to the gay closet and the undocumented closet.

"I've lived my whole life in the Valley," he said. "My home and my friends are here. But going to UCLA gave me the chance to reinvent myself and start over. I met other gays there who were out. In the first few months, I got more involved with campus life, and it was such a relief to just be around other people without having to act like I was straight!" He smiled so wide his face can hardly contain it.

The next step was dealing with his immigration status. His closest friends knew Luis was undocumented, as did his advisor and some of his professors. He started meeting other students who were undocumented, and although it took some time, gradually he began feeling comfortable enough to talk about it. In March 2011, he came out as undocumented for the first time. SFVDT had been formed two months earlier, and even though Luis had never said, "I'm undocumented and unafraid" before, he got his nerve up to do it at a meeting. He told his story in front of everyone, and that opened the door to a whole new family for him.

"Coming out gives you power," he said. "It makes you want to say it. I felt bad that I had been lying for all that time. I couldn't have a boyfriend. I couldn't have a normal social life. I couldn't travel. I didn't have a license. I had to lie about everything, hiding most of my life. I know that the constant lying affected my personality and character. Now I don't want to hide anything. Sometimes I say it just because I like knowing that I can." He gave me a satisfied grin.

Even though Luis has experienced this liberation for himself, he acknowledges that things are not exactly easy for undocuqueers, partly because society is not ready for people to openly say who they are. He knows that at restaurants, the employers know their employees are undocumented, and the staff knows that their bosses know it. You just can't say it. And if you're gay on top of it, things are even harder. Luis doesn't talk about it at all with his parents, but he can talk to his siblings. He doesn't know how to even begin a conversation on the topic with his parents, and he's not sure they want to hear it.

Even though the two identities seem to be unrelated, sometimes they intersect. Then, any undocuqueer has to twice face the consequences for carrying around a double stigma. In Luis's case, his romantic life has been affected by his immigration status. He began a relationship with another UCLA student, but since it took Luis longer to get through school because he had to take time off to work to pay for it, his boyfriend graduated before him and began planning a future that, for now, could not include him. His boyfriend had been considering traveling outside of the country, and Luis did not have a key to unlock that door yet. The relationship ended. Now Luis has a new boyfriend, Ernesto, who was undocumented himself until recently and knows what it's like.

As Dreamers, undocuqueers have some unique disadvantages. For some Dreamers, simply falling in love with a US citizen can resolve all their immigration problems, because through marrying a citizen, they can apply for permanent residency and even citizenship someday. But for those in same-sex relationships, the door stayed firmly shut until June 2013, when the US Supreme Court's decision in *US v. Windsor* cleared the way for same-sex married couples to receive federal benefits. These open an opportunity for mixed immigration-status couples, as the US Citizenship and Immigration Services (USCIS) looks to the state where the marriage was performed to determine whether the couple is eligible for benefits. But at the moment of our conversation, the benefits bestowed upon immigrant spouses of citizens were still completely denied to the undocuqueer community, and for that reason, Jorge told me, it makes sense for LGBT people to be so well represented in the ranks of the Dreamer leadership.

"I don't want to have to pretend to be straight and get into a fake marriage to get my papers," he says. "I'd rather fight on both fronts. Now we are doubly denied an opportunity, but fighting for both can be a double opportunity in itself. If a law is passed for the gay rights movement, we'll have a chance, and if one is passed for immigrant rights, we'll have a chance there, too. When you start fighting for one thing, the door for the other one opens."

I VISITED EL HORMIGUERO for a second time a few months later, after Luis sent me an invitation through a Facebook group to come to the Undocuqueer Healing Oasis. Doing some research on the movement after we first talked, I discovered it had grown to become a national network over the course of just a few months. Many of the local United We Dream chapters included subgroups of members who openly identified as undocuqueer, and they decided to support a national project called the Queer Undocumented Immigrant Project, or QUIP. The event at El Hormiguero would take place on the last Friday in August, and the featured guest would be Jorge, aka Maria sin Papeles. I learned that Jorge had played a fundamental role in building a national undocuqueer network.

While he was in his last semester at Fullerton, Jorge found out about the Orange County Dream Team (OCDT) and discovered the perfect forum for sharing his experiences as a Dreamer. It was 2007, the year he says he consciously merged his two identities as undocumented and queer. The first time he openly declared his undocumented status in public was at an OCDT meeting for potential new members. Breaking down in tears, he had talked about the limitations implicit in not having documentation, his anger and frustration, and the feeling that going to college was a waste if he couldn't get a decent job after he graduated. After that first time came another, and another, and another. Jorge grew stronger the more he talked publicly about his status, even in television interviews, channeling his fear into something positive. Eventually he realized it didn't make sense to be completely open about this aspect of his life, while still hiding another side of himself.

"I felt like I was driving a car and my other identity was sitting next to me," he told me one morning as we talked at the UCLA Labor Center, where some student activist organizations can come to do office work. "I started to notice that some of the other guys in OCDT were queer, too, but they weren't telling their stories. I decided we had to talk about it, so I got my nerve up and started telling my story as a queer."

At first, the group's reaction was not exactly what Jorge had hoped for. Some listened, cautious, while others openly turned their backs on him. But instead of harboring bitterness about it, now Jorge describes it as "a moment of reflection for the organization, to see what they would do with this." Jorge kept on telling his story at meetings, especially when new members joined, and gradually others joined in with their own testimonials. Five years later, OCDT describes itself as "queer inclusive."

Jorge's proudest moment came in March 2011, at the national United We Dream conference in Memphis, Tennessee. More than two hundred Dreamers from across the country came to the event to participate in workshops and training exercises, planning the future of the movement in the wake of Congress's failure to pass the DREAM Act four months earlier. There, he was asked to tell his story to the media. He decided that if he were going to tell his story, it would be the whole thing.

"I started talking about the challenges I had faced as an undocumented immigrant and as a queer, and as I spoke, I watched the audience's reaction, which was very intense, very strong," he says. "But I didn't know if it was because they were uncomfortable or because they were connecting to my story. When I was done I said, 'If any of you here identify as undocumented LGBT [lesbian, gay, bisexual, or transgender], please join us.'"

For several seconds nothing happened. Nothing. Jorge felt his heart stop. In an instant, he had a thought, telling himself it didn't matter what happened, he had to keep right on working with what they had. Suddenly, a young man in the audience stood up. Then another, and another, and another, until there were twenty-five or thirty young people on their feet, coming out of the shadows on two fronts at a national event. The room broke out in thunderous applause, and people were crying and hugging each other.

"I think that was the point when the immigrant movement started going in a new direction and was able to expand into another area," Jorge says. "It was a surprise for members of some groups, because they didn't know any of their members were queer and hadn't felt comfortable enough to tell them. It was a time of reflection, to think about how to change their organizations so the members would feel secure enough to tell their stories there.

"That's where QUIP came from, and that's given all the undocuqueers the chance not just to tell their stories to each other, not just come out to each other, but to create some leadership, to have some visibility outside of our own organization so that our experiences, identities, and priorities will be considered within the political work and campaigns."

The last Friday in August arrived, and El Hormiguero was ready to welcome anybody and everybody to the undocuqueer event. Jorge, wearing jeans and a T-shirt, calm and relaxed as usual, waited to greet people as they arrived. I saw Marcos, the organization's founder, and some other familiar faces, like Agustin, Ernesto, and, of course, Luis.

The mood lighting was dim and inviting. A little dog named Xolotl greeted arrivals as they came inside. Chips and dip and ginger ale were set out on the table. I had brought a tray of *conchas*, or Mexican sweet rolls. Even though people spoke English with one another, they called the rolls *pan*, the Spanish word for bread, asking, "Do you want some *pan?*"

The evening began with a discussion on double identity, being undocumented and being gay. Jorge talked about two concepts and how transitioning from one to the other can help heal and strengthen. The first concept was negotiation, meaning the reaction to situations that force those who are undocumented and queer to negate one, or both, of those identities in order to be able to successfully interact socially. The second concept was navigation, meaning choosing a well-reasoned response to get through those situations in the best way for the person affected. There were plenty of examples: Times when a gay man has to modulate his voice or talk about subjects he normally has no interest in just to "fit in" in a masculine situation. Or the times when a gay woman has to silently tolerate insulting comments about lesbians in order to avoid putting herself in a vulnerable position. And, of course, the many times everyone has to lie whenever a situation comes up alluding to the existence of legal documentation to be in the country.

"Before I got involved in the movement, I would negotiate with myself," Jorge related. "Before going to a meeting or an event I would decide that just for that day I was only going to be undocumented, and another time I would just be queer. It was really hard, but I did it because I didn't have a community or any support.

"Now, because of the work I have done on myself, I have changed this process into a navigation," he says. "I make choices strategically, not painfully; like, it's part of a challenge. I know how to navigate to get resources, to be a better leader, to be a better friend, to get power. When you navigate, you don't force the situation. You are in control, and you get whatever is best for you out of it."

Some nodded in agreement, while others quietly mulled over the idea. That evening's attendees were two women, several men, and two transgendered people who asked to be referred to as "she." When Jorge had finished addressing the group, it was time for everyone to share their experiences. It reminded me of scenes I had seen in movies of Alcoholics Anonymous meetings, but the atmosphere was very warm; there were lots of smiles; and Xolotl the dog had a knack for appearing at just the right moment to break the tension. Some of the group had known one another for a long time, but for others this was their first meeting. I felt like I was witnessing something special, that this would be a real watershed moment for some of them.

I came because I know a have to give my body and my heart a chance to heal. Where should I start? We are programmed by so many circumstances. . . .

—MICHAEL

I was lucky enough to get an office job after graduation. Even when I don't say it, I'm always afraid. It's so weird to go to demonstrations for undocumented people and not be able to tell my coworkers that I am undocumented, even though I know that they know. And on top of that, I'm gay. And on top of that, I'm a woman. And even when I'm working in a nongovernmental organization, I always see sexism. My boss has told me he's homophobic, but he's a powerful old Chicano, and if I challenge him on it that would mean burning my bridges.

—MARGARITA

The main objective of the Chicano movement revolved around the Vietnam War, but nobody added other issues or another agenda, and that was a mistake. They didn't look at the immigration issue again until 2006, with the marches, and that was just because they had to keep selling their books. But Rudy Acuña hasn't included queers in any of the many revised editions of his best seller *Occupied America*. Maybe in 2040 they'll finally talk about rights for fags. I know that's harsh, but it's true.

—MARCO

Sometimes I feel like being undocumented is superimposed over everything else because I'm so aware of it all the time: when I'm out to dinner, when I'm shopping, when I'm with my friends. But I don't want people to see me as either bisexual or undocumented; I want them to see the whole me. That's hard because queer groups don't want to see the undocumented part, and pro-immigrant groups don't want to see our queer identity.

—ROCIO

I feel like society in general is more open to you being undocumented than to you being queer.

—MARGARITA

The two identities do not get mixed in any organization or university. The only space where they get mixed is in the community.

—ERICKA

I was born in the US, but I consider myself undocumented because there is no document that reflects my identity. I have been taking hormones for a long time and I feel like I am halfway there. I don't feel like a man, but I don't feel like a woman yet. But every time I have to fill out some form, I have to choose one. The hardest part has been having to explain to my father, a Colombian and a Catholic, that I'm transgender. That I'm not gay; I'm a woman.

—MICHA

I consider myself a supporter, but I've seen my friends fighting, working so they can go to school later. I see how they've been able to overcome those obstacles and make things happen. That makes me feel blessed to be documented and not have to deal with all that, but we face lots of other kinds of discrimination, and in Hispanic culture it's even worse, so I have had to learn how to define myself: I am a nurse, I'm Latino, I'm fat, and I'm gay.

—GEORGE

People start asking you to divide yourself into pieces, but as undocuqueers, we have to understand those are just parts of broken identities. That's the problem, having events where you have to choose between being Latino or being queer. But we have a lot of little powers: we are Latinos, we are undocumented, we are queer, women; all of that combined together makes us powerful. We understand all the different layers of repression, but we can join them together to make an even more powerful whole.

—MARCOS

Really, we should all give ourselves a round of applause.

—GEORGE

HER BRIGHTLY PAINTED LIPS, exceeding their natural outline, perfectly accentuate Maria sin Papeles's smile when she tells a joke. She speaks mostly in English but saves Spanish for the funniest phrases that really define her personality.

"I just crossed the border and my mama was like, '*Apúrate, cabrona*,' *que el* Deferred Action, *que la Acción Diferida*," Maria says. "I know some of you are thinking, '*Bueno esta qué, ¿es prostituta o qué?*' but I can take it. I'm from Mexico, from Nayarit. *Ay, estos* eyelashes *no me dejan ver nada.* Maria sin Papeles came here to work, *a chingarle.* What do I do? I sell Avon. I have a brother back home, and I take care of him."

Maria sin Papeles grew out of an OCDT initiative in 2009. One day when some of the members were talking, Jorge among them, it occurred to him that since they were working to strengthen the organization's queer identity, it could be a good idea to put on a show with drag queens as a fund-raiser. Jorge presented it as something fun to do, while raising political consciousness at the same time. They did their first event that year, which drew an audience of

150. It has become even larger in subsequent years and is an annual event. At the most recent OCDT show, they raised $1,500.

One time when he was getting ready to go out on stage, applying makeup and adjusting his wig, Jorge thought he should create a character inspired by Mexican popular culture.

"I thought about the characters Thalia played in the telenovelas: Marimar, Maria Mercedes, Maria la del Barrio," he says. "So I decided I would be Maria sin Papeles. The concept has evolved, and I've tried to portray her responsibly, consciously. She's somebody who can talk about things that Jorge might be afraid to. She can be analytical and criticize the work me and my friends do, and she does it very creatively, not negatively, in a way that's not mean, it just makes you think. I wanted to create a character who's vulnerable but not weak. She's someone who we can find in our communities, someone you can identify with."

Maria tells her story, speaking into the microphone. She talks about when she was six years old and hanging around with her best friend, who happened to be named America. She talks about how even more than the little girl herself, she was always interested in her dresses and how she was groomed; Maria shares how her little girlfriends as a child helped her to discover her own femininity. "*Bueno*, I was at the *rancho* then. It was hard being a queer at six years old, all the boys taunting you when they're in groups, *porque* when they're together, they're *bien machitos y bien cabrones*, but when they're alone, [it's] '*Hey, how's it going?*,'" she says in a melodious voice. The audience bursts into laughter.

She goes on: "Coming here tonight was a big transformation for me, from going through the mall, finding these shoes, trying them on, and then the families watching me, and the little kid, 'Mama, *mamá, mira, mira,*' y la señora, '*Ay m'ijo no mires, vente*' ["don't look; let's go"]. I saw all of you here tonight, everybody so serious with their diplomas during the day, but at night, *bien locas*. Doesn't matter. No one's gonna ask you for your papers on the dance floor . . . not yet."

Before she finishes her presentation, Maria dedicates her appearance that night to women everywhere "and to my mother, because she let me wear a corset." She asks everyone to stand in a circle, and the DJ plays the first song. The Dreamers step onto the dance floor; the guys dance with Maria, and the girls hug her. Roadblocks demanding licenses, astronomical tuition bills, the risk of deportation, and Washington, DC's laws are all very far away. Just for today, everybody is exactly who they dream to be, because nobody asks to see your papers on the dance floor . . . at least not yet.

CHAPTER 10

---◆---

#BRINGTHEMHOME

SUNSETS IN THE ARIZONA desert are spectacular. Dry, rough grass covers the ground for as far as the eye can see and suddenly dims in shadows. The clouds part and offer a glimpse of clear sky turning a brilliant golden-orange at dusk. The sun dips below the desolate horizon, and everything from the scrubby desert floor to the wide-open sky seems to be aflame.

The Eloy Detention Center seems to be burning too. The modern building, surrounded by three fences topped with barbed wire, has a particular design feature that could be either thoughtful or horribly cruel: clear fiberglass windows facing west. For the duration of their confinement, which could last for days, weeks, or months, prisoners can look out and see the sun set on the outside, day after day after day.

Eloy is one of six detention centers in Arizona operated by the Corrections Corporation of America, a for-profit company that manages most privatized prisons in the United States on a concessionary basis. Four of those centers, including Eloy, are strategically located within an area of two square miles, between Phoenix, the state capital, and Tucson—and one hundred miles from the Mexican border crossing in Nogales. Eloy has 1,596 beds for men and women who committed the offense of being on the northern side of the border without a piece of paper. But on June 22, 2013, there was a blip in the usual monotonous functioning of the arrest-and-deport machinery. That morning, inhabitants in both towns that share the name Nogales, on the northern and southern sides of the border, looked on as nine young people dressed in graduation caps and gowns marched determinedly from the Mexican side and attempted to cross into the United States, asserting that it was their country.

The five women and four men represented almost five hundred thousand of their peers who grew up on American soil without documentation and at some point as adults had to return to the country where they were born, which for most is Mexico. Like Nancy Landa, many were forced to go back because of a deportation order. Others simply decided to go back on their own, faced with the harsh reality of having little opportunity in the United States. Some others had to go back because of a family emergency or to be reunited with family members who had been deported. They all have one thing in common: they are all Dreamers who could still be living in the country they think of as home if they had been in the United States when Deferred Action went into effect.

The group of nine waiting at the crossing station fall into that category. Some have been living in Mexico for years, others a few months or even just a few days. All nine understand very well that attempting to cross back into the country they consider their own through an official point of entry and openly acknowledging their undocumented status means they will be detained indefinitely. All nine are willing to take the risk.

THE BRING THEM HOME campaign is an action orchestrated by the National Immigrant Youth Alliance (NIYA), a network composed of DreamActivist members and their leader, Mo Abdollahi, and other activist groups of undocumented young people across the country. After carrying out approximately twenty civil disobedience actions between 2010 and 2013, they decided to extend their efforts beyond the border, seeking not only to prevent any Dreamers from being deported but also to enable those who were outside the country to return, using the two legal strategies that could apply to them: soliciting a humanitarian visa or requesting political asylum.

After I met with Mo in Alabama in 2011 and then in Arizona in 2012, we were in almost constant communication. He gave me frequent updates on his organization's plans and on happenings throughout the network. In June 2013 Mo sent me a message letting me know he was going to be in Los Angeles and asking if we could get together. We made plans to meet for dinner.

Halfway through the meal, while we were talking about the immigration reform initiative being debated at the time, Mo asked me, "What would you think if some of our group went to Mexico and tried to come back through a border crossing?"

At first I thought he was joking. But as he explained the plan, I realized he was very serious. He had been consulting with lawyers for the previous few months, exploring the possibilities. Three "high-profile" Dreamers would go to Mexico and meet up with five others who had been there already, and then as a group they would all try to cross the border into the United States legally.

"We're going to put Obama's deportation policies to the test," Mo commented, as a waiter brought us our shrimp tacos. "We'll look for Dreamers in high-risk situations in Mexico, who have reason to fear for their lives if they are outside of the US. We think the best place to do it is Arizona, because we have supporters there and the issue gets a lot of attention, but we haven't decided on which border crossing yet. If everything goes according to plan, we could do it in mid-June."

To devise their legal strategy, NIYA and DreamActivist had tapped Margo Cowan, an attorney in her fifties with a friendly expression, a penetrating gaze, and a ferocious will. A public defender in Pima County, Arizona, Cowan earned her law degree in the 1980s. An expert in immigration law, Cowan specializes in undocumented immigrants and refugees and is a cofounder of No More Deaths, a group that aims to reduce the number of deaths among undocumented immigrants trying to cross the southwestern desert. Cowan agreed to work with the Dreamers pro bono. Cowan's legal strategy was to have the Dreamers first apply for humanitarian visas, which are rarely granted. Because this request would most likely be denied, she also prepared applications for asylum for each of the Dreamers, asserting that they had "credible fear" of threat if they remained outside of the United States.

Under international law, when a person requests asylum at a port of entry, that country is obligated to consider the request and decide whether the case warrants a hearing, where evidence will be presented. There are two processes for this in the United States. One is known as Affirmative Asylum, which takes place when a person is already in the United States—if they have entered with a visa, for example. The other is called Defensive Asylum, when the person tries to enter the United States from another country at a port of entry. In the latter case, the solicitant is usually taken to a detention center and held there until a judge determines whether an official asylum case should be opened. This first phase can last two to four weeks, although in some cases, months have gone by before a judge has made a decision. If the judge decides the applicant may fall under the "credible fear" category, then the case moves forward and the applicant must present proof and undergo extensive interviews. Because of the huge backlog in the courts, this second phase can drag on for four or five years, or even more. In most cases, the applicant is released from detention and may remain in the United States legally while the case is being resolved. So if the Dreamers, who had lived in the United States undocumented for years, could successfully demonstrate they had "credible fear," they would then be able to live in the United States legally, with documentation, for at least as long as it took to decide their case. And if the case was decided in their favor, they could have legal status permanently. The only risk was if they had to spend an extended time in detention, which could become unbearable, but they all said they were willing to take the chance.

In mid-July, NIYA/DreamActivist announced that the crossing attempt would take place in Nogales and eight Dreamers who had undergone training would participate. Later one more person joined the group, which soon became known as the #Dream9 of the #BringThemHome movement on social networking sites. Three of the nine, Lizbeth Mateo, Marco Saavadra, and Lulu Martinez, all members of DreamActivist, left the United States to meet up with the others. During a conversation on the phone, Mo emphasized to me that the premise of DreamActivist was that members would not ask others to do anything they were not willing to do themselves. Of the other six—Adriana Diaz, Ceferino Santiago, Luis Leon, Maria Peniche, Mario Felix, and Claudia Amaro—some had been deported to Mexico, and others had been forced to leave the United States for family reasons or because they could no longer attend school.

"I know they're going to think I'm crazy for doing this, for leaving the United States," Lizbeth said in a video recorded in the Mexican state of Oaxaca, where she had traveled a few days before the action to visit her grandmother for the first time since she and her parents and siblings had migrated to the United States. "But I think it's even crazier that I have had to wait fifteen years to see my family again. I'm doing this not only for my family but for the thousands who have been deported—1.7 million people . . . and those 1.7 million are not the only ones affected. Their families are affected too, like mine was."

CLAUDIA AMARO IS SOMETHING of an expert in starting over from square one. She had to do it when she was just ten when her father was murdered, turning her life upside down. She had to start over again at thirteen, when her mother decided to move with Claudia and her three sisters to the United States, to escape Mexico's escalating violence. The life she knew ended abruptly for a third time when she was thirty and her husband received an order of deportation, sending the two of them and their son, Yamil, a US citizen, back to a Mexico she felt no connection to. At thirty-seven, with nothing to lose and hoping to get back a little of what she had lost, in July 2013 Claudia set off on the journey that would change her life for the fourth time. She prepared to be locked up in a detention center for however long it took, and wearing a graduation cap and gown, she walked up to the border station in Nogales with the eight other Dreamers.

The eldest of four girls, Claudia was born in Tijuana, Mexico. When she was ten her family moved to the state of Durango, where her father was murdered under murky circumstances that have never been fully investigated by law enforcement. In the months following her father's killing, his murderers began harassing the family. So when Claudia was about to turn thirteen, her mother decided to take her four daughters to live in Colorado, in the United States.

Claudia first got in touch with me through Facebook in early July. She was aware that for the previous few months I had been following DreamActivist's civil disobedience actions, and she wanted to know if I could give her some more information on the group and about Mo, with whom she had also gotten in contact. A few weeks after that exchange, she wrote to me again to tell me she had decided to be a part of the group that would try to enter the United States in Nogales. The day before she left the town of Torreón, where she was living, we talked on the phone, and she told me about her life, about how hard it had been to leave all her friends when she was a young teenager, what it had been like to suddenly find herself in a new country, still grieving the loss of her father, and about the challenges she had faced in Colorado.

"There weren't many Hispanics back then," she said. "There were only three or four Mexicans from Mexico in our whole school and the first year was really hard: We didn't know the language. I was bullied. I didn't eat anything at all at school for days because I didn't know the system; I didn't know to just pick up a tray in the cafeteria and serve myself."

When she was seventeen the family moved again, to Wichita, Kansas. There, Claudia began to build the foundation of what would be her adult life. She refers to her time there as "the best years of my life."

"For the first time, I felt at home. I didn't miss Mexico anymore. My sisters and I formed a youth group at our church. I met my husband there, and we got married in 1998, when I was twenty-three. In 2000 Yamil was born."

Everything was going fine until she got a call in 2005. Her husband had been pulled over on a routine traffic stop and had been detained. Claudia had to go to the police station where he was being held.

"I told them I was his wife and asked what I had to do. They took me into a little room to interrogate me, and then they handcuffed me and brought me to immigration. They released us on bail and the process went on until December. But then in January 2006 they issued an order of deportation for my husband. When we protested that we had a six-year-old son who was a US citizen, the judge said he was still little, he could adapt to life in Mexico," Claudia remembered. On the other end of the phone I could hear her voice tighten as she tried to hold back tears. "We couldn't work at all during the nine months it took for the case to be decided. We lost the house we had been paying off, the car, everything. We went back to Mexico with one foot still back in this country."

Claudia had to repeat the painful process of adaptation she had had to go through when she first came to the United States, but this time it was twice as hard. She and her husband had to adjust to a country that didn't feel like theirs anymore, and their son had to adapt to a whole new world. Yamil was held back a year at school because he didn't speak Spanish well. They found a private school where he would get more individual attention but even that did not spare him from being jeered and teased by the other kids for being American. Claudia and her husband had to present a formal complaint after six other boys beat Yamil because of where he was from.

"They called him *pocho*; they made fun of him. In first grade he was really depressed. We had to take him to a therapist," she said. "The therapist told us that part of the problem was that my husband and I had not completely accepted that we now lived in Mexico and that was our life now, but how can we? We've been here for seven years now and we haven't been able to get used to it. I don't feel American or Mexican, I feel like a person who has a home in Wichita. That's where my family and my past is."

As Claudia told me her story, I could hear the anger and frustration rising in her voice. She told me that three months earlier her family had been robbed at gunpoint. Thirteen-year-old Yamil had seen a gunman hold a pistol to his father's head. After that the boy did not want to leave the house.

"The first time I left Mexico because my father was murdered and the authorities didn't do anything. I don't want my son to live like that. I want to go home, I want my son to have the life he has every right to have as a US citizen, because he's gone through some awful things he never should have had to go through here. I'm going to the United States, to the land of immigrants, the land that sees me as one of its children. I love the Mexican people, I admire how hardworking they are, but there are stars and stripes in my heart. I'm going home."

On June 22, dressed in graduation caps and gowns, Claudia and the other eight Dreamers linked arms and walked up to the border station in Nogales, smiling brightly. A group of supporters walked with them, chanting, "Undocumented and unafraid!" and "Bring them home!" Yamil was with them. On the other side of the border, Claudia's mother waited for her grandson. He entered his home country without any problem. Claudia gazed at her son one more time before she presented herself to the authorities. The nine Dreamers were handcuffed, escorted into a van, and taken to the Eloy Detention Center.

It was Monday afternoon, August 5. As they have every day since the nine Dreamers were taken to Eloy, supporters held a vigil in front of the fence that separated those detained inside from the outside world of brilliant sunsets. Dust from the road billowed around cars as they pulled in from Phoenix or Tucson, after long, rough rides, finally arriving on the street ironically named Sunshine Boulevard.

On this day, thirteen people formed a circle and held hands as the sun set. One began reciting a prayer and the others joined in. They prayed for the nine to be released so they could go home soon and be with the families that awaited them here in the United States. Those holding vigil counted the days until the asylum cases for the nine could formally begin. Family and friends closed their eyes and joined in the group prayer, sharing their collective anxiety. Suddenly they heard cracking sounds coming from some distance away. They turned to face the prison and waved their arms. Though they knew the detainees could not hear them from so far away, that their voices would be lost in the desert, they shouted encouraging words anyway. The percussive sounds grew louder.

"It's the prisoners," one of those participating in the vigil explained. "The ones who can see us get excited when somebody comes here, since nobody ever comes here. One of the Dreamers told us on the phone the other day that the other prisoners like people to come gather here, because it's like we're serenading them."

A few hours after the vigil, members of DreamActivist got a call from Cowan, their attorney, informing them the request for political asylum had been tentatively granted for seven of the nine Dreamers. Now the long evaluation process would begin and they expected immigration authorities to announce their release in a few hours. Only Marco and Lizbeth were left. When a judge decides whether to let an asylum case go forward, he or she must determine whether the applicant can be released from detention while the case makes its way through the system. Because holding anyone in detention for any length of time is extremely expensive, in most cases a temporary work permit is granted, allowing the applicant to be released and get a job while the case is being resolved (depending on an applicant's profile and whether the case has received any media attention). So, on the outside, their supporters prepared for the Dreamers to be released.

The next day, Mo, nervous and irritable, took part in a demonstration along with other protest leaders in Phoenix. That same day President Obama was visiting a school there, and DreamActivist decided to publicly denounce the administration's deportation policy. Amid a whirlwind of press interviews and chanted slogans, Mo's cell phone rang. He quickly answered it and walked some distance away to talk where he could hear. He came back a few minutes later, beaming: "That was Lizbeth. They're releasing all nine."

After days of putting on a stoic, serious front for the media, everyone started hugging, happy and amazed at the outcome. By following a careful legal strategy that took advantage of existing immigration laws, developing a targeted, aggressive media campaign, and relying on the large network of supporters it had cultivated over the previous three years, DreamActivist had succeeded in having nine of its undocumented members leave the United States, come back through an official immigration border station, and stay legally for at least a few years. A handful of young people had managed to accomplish in just two weeks what congressional representatives, activists, and lawyers had been trying to do for two decades. DreamActivist was making history. Next to me was Benito Miller, who just a few months earlier had trained the group of protesters in nonviolent civil disobedience before the action in Phoenix. Smiling broadly, staring off into the distance, he said softly to no one in particular, "We just officially became 'coyotes.'"

The #Dream9 were released on August 7 at four o'clock in the afternoon. After one last visit to the Nogales border station, this time on the US side, they all headed for home.

A FEW HOURS BEFORE they were released I talked with Elvia, Claudia's mother. Elvia lives in Kansas and took care of Yamil for the two weeks that Claudia was in custody. She spoke about how brave her daughter was for leaving the life she had worked so hard to create in Mexico and about how stressful the past few weeks had been.

"And you know what else really worries me? Thinking about the other moms, like Lizbeth's mother in Los Angeles or Adriana's, who's on the other side in Mexico, in Nogales," Elvia said. "They can't be here close by, talking with the lawyer. Can you imagine the stress? And knowing your daughter is in there, all alone?"

On the day the #Dream9 were released, a horde of reporters gathered amid television cameras in the parking lot of the Greyhound bus terminal in Tucson, waiting. Suddenly, off in the distance, five silhouettes appearing to wear caps and gowns came into view, walking toward them. It was the women; the men would arrive a few minutes later. People in the parking lot started running toward the women. Elvia went along, and I decided to follow her so I could see her hug her daughter. I was surprised to see her first hurry to wrap her arms around Adriana, who burst into tears, overcome with emotion. Elvia stretched out one arm and pulled Lizbeth to her, kissing her hair and comforting her. I remembered our talk earlier: Lizbeth's mom was in Los Angeles and Adriana's was in Mexico. Only after helping these two girls, all alone, to feel at home did she then go to hug her own daughter.

ADRIANA GIL RESTS HER HAND on the fence that separates Mexico and the United States. Pressed against one of the poles, she brings her face as close to the metal as she can. Surrounded by reporters, she says softly, "I love you so much." "I love you too," Maria Antonia, her mother, quickly replies from the other side of the fence, her hand mirroring her daughter's.

Although the land on either side of this stretch of the border shares the same name, they are different worlds. Migrants ejected by a country that refuses to acknowledge how essential they are land in Nogales, Mexico, in the state of Sonora. Nogales, Arizona, is the point of entry to the ever-tantalizing American Dream.

Adriana came to the United States in her mother's arms when she was four months old. Originally from Mexico City, the family settled in Phoenix. Adriana graduated from high school with honors in 2010 but since she could not go on to college because of the restrictions placed on undocumented immigrants in Arizona, she decided to return to Mexico to continue her studies. Her mother went with her. Three months after she left the United States, in June 2012, President Obama announced the Deferred Action program. Adriana's whole world fell in on her.

She encountered bureaucratic difficulties that made it impossible for her to enroll in college in Mexico—a problem Dreamers commonly face when they go there thinking it will be easier to pursue a higher education. So mother and daughter decided to go to stay in Nogales to be close to the border and look into the possibility of getting a border visa, or BCC, the document issued by the US government that authorizes Mexican border residents to visit the United

States. With this document, they can remain there up to thirty days and travel no more than twenty-five miles beyond the border. That's where Adriana joined the #Dream9. Seventeen days later, after two weeks in prison, she said good-bye to her mother through the gaps in a metal fence and went back to Phoenix, her home.

The highway running from Nogales to Phoenix goes right by Eloy. Outside the detention center, under the watchful eyes of hundreds of undocumented prisoners, the sun starts to set and the desert blazes once again.

IT'S SIX IN THE EVENING on a Saturday, and Nuevo Laredo, in the Mexican state of Tamaulipas, is practically deserted. There are no crowds of weekend shoppers anymore, because Nuevo Laredo has been scarred by violence. Only a few businesses are open, mostly small markets or restaurants. The streets of the city are rougher, dirtier, and dustier the farther they are from the center. On one particularly weather-beaten street is La Casa del Migrante Nazareth, a shelter run by Scalabrinian missionaries that every day takes in migrants just deported from the United States or those in need of a little rest before they attempt to cross, after long journeys from other Mexican states or Central America. The shelter has 140 beds. On the last weekend of September 2013, thirty of them are occupied by Dreamers.

A metal door opens, and a man with a warm expression lets me in only after confirming I have permission to be there. His name is Tino. He is on staff there and seems to take pride in his work. He asks me to wait for someone to come out. The large vestibule, bathed in light streaming in through the windows covered with security bars, has a solemn air. A photo of Father Giovanni Scalabrini is the focal point. A few people pass by and see me there, looking over their shoulders at me again. I ask Tino how many people are staying there now, and he says there are about forty migrants aside from the Dreamers. "But it's not night yet, soon around forty more will come," he says casually. "They keep coming at night because that's when the deportations happen."

I tell Tino that according to international agreements, the authorities are not allowed to leave deported migrants at the border late at night. He looks at me as if he can't believe how naïve I am.

"Sometimes they come here at one in the morning. When they get to the border there's nobody there waiting for them, not even just to give them information," he explains. "Some go to the bus terminal—they're the lucky ones. But others just stay here. They are the most vulnerable."

Then Benito comes out to greet me. In his twenties, with a pale complexion, curly blond hair, and a calm demeanor, Benito is a DreamActivist leader who has accompanied Mo on several of the group's actions. We met once in Phoenix, and his participation had been key a month and a half earlier in Nogales. Now here we were again, along the border dividing Tamaulipas from Texas.

Following the resounding success of the #Dream9 action, Benito is in charge of training the thirty Dreamers in this shelter so they will know what to say to the authorities, understand the legal implications of their cases, be able to speak effectively to the media, and be prepared for the hardships they will face if they are arrested. This new, larger group, also made up of young undocumented immigrants who grew up in the United States but had to leave the country, will get to know and learn to trust and rely on one another, because from now on they will be like family. Their lives will forever be divided into "before" and "after" Laredo.

Benito says hello and soon hands me over to Sandra Jara, one of the women in the group, who shows me around, introduces me to the other Dreamers and explains the shelter's rules. I greet her like she's an old friend, because just a few days earlier I had interviewed her via Skype and she had told me her story.

Originally from Peru, the only non-Mexican participating in the action, Sandra migrated to the United States and initially settled in Los Angeles with her mother when she was fifteen. After she went through a period of adjustment, like all young immigrants, Sandra and her mother moved to Alhambra, California. When it was time to apply to college, Sandra realized that she could not continue her education and she couldn't get a job, either, because she lacked the necessary documentation. Then she tried to figure out a way to go to school in Spain. She returned to her native Lima to apply for a student visa. But her visa application was denied and Sandra's plans for a career were cut off. On top of that, she was separated from her mother and living in a society that did not accept her because she is gay. For all of these reasons, Sandra decided to join the #Dream30, the second round of #BringThemHome.

Wandering through the labyrinthine Casa del Migrante, one hears many stories. There are common rooms and private rooms, where talks are given on AIDS and HIV, on hope and danger, courage and faith. Men sit on the beige tiled floor, waiting for dinner time. Most have sunburned faces, wearing clothes that have seen better days. These men are tired and some are plainly desperate. One offers me a wide, toothless smile. Another watches me from a corner; he has a broken leg. He is from Veracruz and has a daughter who is a US citizen, waiting for him on the other side. He is desperate to cross: a year and a half ago he had to return to Mexico because of a family emergency, and he has not been able to get back. The previous Friday he had tried; he was running just north of the border when he fell and was caught.

It's 101 degrees and humid, typical weather for this area in late September. The shelter has semiprivate rooms for women with two or four cots. Men stay in larger rooms on the upper floor with eight cots to a room. The air smells stale, a bit rank, like people in close quarters—"like feet," one of the men describes it to me later. But every cot is neatly made up, and everyone's belongings are tucked away in bags and backpacks.

Sandra explains that for most of the day the shelter is empty. In the morning the men and women staying there go out to work—many of them want to return to the United States and they need to save some money. They come back at four o'clock; dinner is at six. The shelter is so neat and clean because everyone must follow the rules. Everyone eats together, sitting at tables with their meals already served on plates. Before they start eating they say a prayer, and when dinner is over they volunteer to sweep the floor, wash the dishes, and scrub the pans. Everyone helps fold up the tables and chairs and put them away. The Dreamers staying at the shelter that weekend are not exempt from the chores, although they are allowed to stay inside during the day and they are allowed to use cell phones, a privilege the others do not have for their own security. Tamaulipas has become one of the most dangerous states in Mexico, where migrants are kidnapped by criminal groups and cartels. By forbidding the use of cell phones they avoid the chance of being followed through GPS or other smartphone features.

That Saturday night after dinner, the Dreamers have a training session. Sitting across from each other in pairs, they role-play giving an interview to a reporter. They are taught which way of speaking will best transmit their message and also which words and phrases they should avoid. They learn about what their body language and facial expressions communicate and how to modulate their tone of voice—the stronger, the better.

Later, the training focuses on the actual border crossing station where they will attempt to gain entry into the United States. Benito shows them a map of the area and points out exactly where in Nuevo Laredo they will start to walk—two blocks from the border station—and where the bridge is. He tells them each to carry four Mexican pesos so they can pay the fee to walk across the pedestrian bridge connecting to Laredo. He explains that all calls placed from inside the detention center will be recorded and that they should not discuss any details of their case, not even with their families. They already know that they should wear a long-sleeved shirt, jeans or cotton pants, and comfortable shoes with no laces. They know they should not wear contact lenses, just glasses, and that any belongings that get confiscated when they enter the detention center will be returned to them upon their release, except perhaps their identification.

While Benito talks, one by one the Dreamers are ushered into another room to record their video testimonials, which will be uploaded to YouTube the next day, as has been done for previous actions. Before they go off to bed they practice the slogans they will shout as they attempt to cross the border.

◆

IT'S WEDNESDAY AFTERNOON, and things are quiet at the shelter. There were torrential rainstorms in the morning, which may explain why not as many reporters as they had hoped for have showed up to cover the story. There are a television reporter, a couple of reporters from radio stations, and a few others. After the rain stops, the Dreamers go out into the courtyard, where there are washtubs and clotheslines for doing laundry. A small dog with a yellow coat splashes in the puddles.

Benito forges ahead. He is accompanied by David Bennion, the lawyer in charge of the legal team handling all the cases for the #Dream30. They have folders full of forms and paperwork, and between the two of them they gather any missing signatures, verify important data, and make copies of passports and ID cards. The Dreamers make last-minute phone calls to parents, girlfriends and boyfriends, and siblings waiting for them on the other side and friends organizing events to support them. At ten o'clock that night all their personal belongings, including their phones, will be put into Ziploc bags labeled with their names. Kept safe in a large box, the bags of belongings will be redistributed when—if all goes as hoped—they are released on the US side of the border with political asylum cases pending.

It's well after midnight when they finally get to bed. Barely four hours later they are up having breakfast, saying good-bye to supporters, and hugging one another. They are known as the #Dream30, but really they number more: twenty-nine young adults, four of them minors, and three parents accompanying their children. There's also Elsy, an undocumented Honduran woman who is the mother of Valeria, a disabled four-year-old girl and US citizen. Benito met them just the day before in the shelter. After briefly consulting with the rest of the group he decided to invite them to participate in the action.

Dressed in caps and gowns or T-shirts openly declaring their undocumented status, the thirty-four will march together to the border station that morning. Just then, none of them could predict that eight hours later Elsy and Valeria would be released in the United States with a humanitarian visa for Elsy, and that the next day the four minors would be released from custody along with their parents. They didn't know that in three days the rest of them would be taken to a detention center in El Paso, Texas, where they would be held for weeks. They would be kept together, separated by gender, but would not be allowed contact with any other detainees. That morning they had no way of knowing that while they were in detention the US government would experience a shutdown, which meant that all the phone calls their supporters made to immigration authorities demanding their release would go unanswered. They didn't know that in the following days, streets in major cities across the country would be filled with protesters demanding immigration reform, with some calling specifically for their release. They didn't know that two months later six of them would have their petitions for asylum denied and be deported but that the rest would be released, with legal documentation, in the United States.

Moments before leaving the shelter the Dreamers form a circle and with their arms around one another they say one last prayer together, some weeping.

"We are a family and we don't have borders," Benito reminds them. "Our home is where we feel at home. We are going to create a moral crisis, and US society is going to have to take a hard look at itself and ask themselves if they want to be a just society or not."

The circle of Dreamers rallies one more time:

"Where are we going?" one shouts out.

"We're going home!" the rest shout back.

Single-file, squinting in the sunlight, the #Dream30 go out into the street, about to begin their journey home.

———◆———

THE FIGHT FOR THEIR DREAMS

THE LAST FEW WEEKS of 2012 were very busy for the Dreamer community. In early October, many of the first to have applied for Deferred Action began receiving their documents, including some of the Dreamers I had gotten to know over the previous year and a half. Through their posts on social networks, I saw how thrilled they were to finally have permission to work and to have a Social Security number. Many of them also began to reap the benefits of the California DREAM Act, so they now had a real path to a higher education, and the opportunities for employment after graduation suddenly multiplied.

One of the first people I interviewed for this book was Elioenai Santos, whom I spoke with at California State University, Northridge, in July 2011. At the time, Elioenai had said, "If the DREAM Act is passed in the next few months, I have a future. If it's not, I'm going to have to fight for my future." Since applying for Deferred Action, Elioenai has worked as a journalist for various media outlets for more than a year. Luis, the young man from the San Fernando Valley who had to drop out of school for two terms to work at a restaurant to save up enough money to pay his tuition, received financial aid, and graduated in 2013. Edith, from Dreams To Be Heard at CSUN, got her permission to work and is now a high school teacher. Viridiana, one of the DreamActivists arrested in Phoenix, wrote on her Facebook page, "It feels good to start getting job offers."

All the emotional highs and lows and little victories of this generation are posted for all to see on Facebook's virtual walls. "Sixteen years ago, I worked as a gardener in this office building," one man wrote. "Now I have my own office here. Thanks, Obama."

In spite of this, the bits of good news finally trickling in after so many years of struggle have not been enough and have not solved the underlying problem. Barack Obama has constantly been sending messages to the Dreamers, but his administration's policies have not changed, especially with respect to deportations, which passed the two million mark in 2014. On January 10, 2013, just days from Obama taking the oath of office for a second term, Erika Andiola, a high-profile, tenacious Dreamer activist from Arizona, got the dreaded news that all Dreamers know can come at any time but never want to hear: her mother, Maria Arreola, and her brother, Heriberto Andiola, had been arrested by immigration officials. Erika immediately recorded and uploaded to the Internet an emotional video explaining what had happened and urging the community to start making calls and sending messages to immigration authorities demanding that their deportations be stopped. Erika is a well-known activist leader, so by the next day her plea was getting results. Dozens of organizations had pledged their support, and DreamActivist had gathered signatures requesting that immigration authorities make use of their powers of discretion to release Maria and Heriberto, a power the group has successfully had exercised on their behalf in many of their protests.

A few hours later, Erika announced that her mother and brother had been released. According to her Facebook posts, the bus transporting them along with other deportees was already on its way to Tijuana when the driver got a call ordering him to stop. Erika thanked everyone who had helped and acknowledged that her family was free because of the influence that DreamActivist had brought to bear, while also wondering what had become of the other people on that bus and their children and families.

While the Deferred Action program has been a victory for the Dreamers, and in 2014 a mechanism for its renewal went into effect, it is only a temporary measure and should not be prolonged for an extended period. Only 600,000 of the 1.7 million people eligible for the program have enrolled in it. Those who have enrolled now have a Social Security number and work permit, but their legal status is still in limbo because it doesn't provide them with any way to become permanent residents and includes no pathway to citizenship. On top of that, while they may now have the possibility of a more stable life, in many cases their parents or siblings are still waiting for a reform that will offer a solution. So Deferred Action is bittersweet. Erick, a Dreamer who received his work permit in 2013, wrote on his Facebook page: "It's like being in the middle of a rainstorm with your family, and you're the only one with an umbrella."

WHEN OBAMA'S BID FOR reelection was fast approaching, many analysts feared that large numbers of Latinos would stay away from the polls, reacting to the lack of progress on immigration reform and the brisk pace of deportations. Most Latinos did not want to vote for the Republican candidate, but they felt betrayed by the broken promises of their "Deporter in Chief." In that climate, some activists set to work reminding voters that, historically, whenever a measure supporting immigrants had passed in the United States, it was during a president's second term in office. That was because the immigration issue inevitably unleashed so much controversy that merely bringing it up during a president's first term could cost him the reelection.

Obama entered the White House at a difficult time, faced with a recession, two wars under way, and a health-care system in urgent need of reform. The political capital that had gotten him elected was judiciously administered by the president and his team. Obama's first priority was to work with Congress to pass a package that would stop the country's economic free fall and find a way out of the recession. Then came the tremendously challenging, combative negotiations to pass health-care reform and the formulation of a plan to withdraw troops from Iraq. Adding one more issue on top of all of that, immigration reform, would have exhausted whatever political capital the president may have had left, may not have been sufficient to get anything passed, and very well may have cost him reelection. In that sense, some analysts interpreted Obama's announcement of the Deferred Action program as a campaign strategy and a knowing wink to the Latino community.

Once Obama won his bid for a second term in November 2012, the winks stopped and seemed to be replaced by concrete actions. In his first speech after the election, the president directly referred to the need for immigration reform. And on January 28, eight senators making up a bipartisan commission announced their initiative to draft and pass legislation. The next day, Obama made a statement about the urgent need to get the measure passed. The Senate measure, which prioritized shoring up border security over granting legal status to undocumented immigrants, was passed in the first half of 2013, only to languish in the House of Representatives. By mid-2014, hopes for comprehensive immigration reform had faded, and the most optimistic groups were betting on piecemeal legislation, with different legislative measures that would grant legal status to specific groups, such as farmworkers or Dreamers, supported by certain sectors of the economy that would benefit from legalizing that particular subset of the undocumented population. This approach would not change the status of the majority of undocumented immigrants, leaving them vulnerable to abuse and at risk of deportation.

Many people in the United States without legal status have lived on the far margins of the law because the law simply lacks a mechanism to officially recognize and include them in the country's institutional life. They cannot be legally employed, and they cannot legally drive a car to get to work; in some states they are ineligible for basic services because they do not have a Social Security number. But, of course, it is well known that they do work, drive, and get social services, and that is the way it has been for years. The American public is not only aware of this, but they take full advantage of it: The employer who pays a lower wage to, or does not withhold taxes for, an undocumented worker. The car dealer who sells a vehicle to someone without a license or someone who is uninsured. The insurance agent who sells a policy to someone who does not qualify for it. The service provider who provides a service to someone knowing full well the Social Security number supplied is false. And everyone who in some way benefits from these economic exchanges. It's a system that functions outside the law but is badly broken when seen from within the confines of the law. A system that posits that whoever breaks the law once will continue to break it. A society that knows the system that is in place and exploits it for its own benefit.

IN MID-2013, WHEN THE Spanish-language edition of this book was about to be published in Mexico, I found out about a project that was just getting off the ground, which would turn out to be a natural extension of my work with the Dreamer groups in the United States. *Los Otros Dreamers* ("The other dreamers") was created by Jill Anderson, an academic, and Nin Solís, a photographer. The project started with a crowdfunding campaign on Kickstarter, raising money to publish a book. Published in the fall of 2014, *Los Otros Dreamers* is a collective portrait of life in Mexico for young people who, like Nancy Landa or the #BringThemHome participants, were forced to return to Mexico, by the authorities or for personal reasons, after growing up in the United States. The book presents twenty-six stories written by their protagonists in English, Spanish, or Spanglish—however the authors were most comfortable expressing themselves—and their translations. Naturally, one of the stories included is Nancy Landa's.

As soon as I heard about the project I got in touch with Jill and Nin, and the first chance I got I went to Mexico City to meet with them. We met at a bar across from the Monument to the Revolution in the heart of the city and just steps away from the headquarters of TeleTech. A customer service company whose clients are United States businesses, TeleTech has call centers in Mexico to take advantage of low labor costs. The company employs young adults who, like the Dreamers, had been brought to the United States as small children, were raised as Americans, and then were forced to return to Mexico as adults. Fully bilingual and bicultural, these workers are able to talk to customers calling from the United States in their own language, easily understanding all their slang and regional accents. These employees would probably have a hard time joining the workforce in Mexico if it were not for companies who hire them specifically because they are bilingual, binational, and bicultural.

Jill, in her thirties with straight, light-brown hair falling to her shoulders and a ready smile, decided to talk to some of them one day and found out that some had been deported. They didn't all comfortably fit the definition of a "Dreamer," the model student who longs to go to college; some had been deported for gang-related activity or had been in prison. Originally from Austin, Texas, Jill came to the capital of Mexico in 2007 on a scholarship from the Center for Research on North America at the Universidad Nacional Autonoma de Mexico (UNAM) and has studied the phenomenon of Dreamers returning to Mexico ever since. According to data she has gathered, over the past ten years more than half a million Dreamers have been deported. They end up getting jobs in places like the call centers, where the wage of 45 pesos an hour, less than four dollars, is still more than the average wage for young adult workers in Mexico City. Since it would be very difficult to land a job at other companies in Mexico—because their college degrees are not recognized there, they are not (for the most part) proficient in Spanish, and they are not familiar with the culture—their opportunities for professional development and career advancement are severely limited.

Nancy Landa is an exceptional case. In 2012 Nancy decided she wanted to go back to school to earn a master's degree, and she tried to find a program, but it turned out to be impossible. The Mexican universities did not recognize the diplomas she had earned in the United States. They required her to earn equivalent degrees in Mexico first, which would have meant making a ridiculous investment of time and effort. In an entry on her blog *Mundo Citizen*, which she started soon after her deportation, Nancy chronicles how she decided to look for opportunities beyond Mexico. After applying for several financial aid programs, and even collecting some money on her own through a crowdfunding website, Nancy enrolled in a master's program in global migration studies at University College London in September 2013. In a column on the right of her blog page, Nancy installed a countdown clock, marking how much time she has left until ten years has passed since her deportation. As "punishment," the US government bars any deportee from applying for a visa to enter the country for ten years.

ON APRIL 25, 2014, Nancy returned to California State University, Northridge, her alma mater. She didn't go back exactly the way she would have liked, and the way she most likely will some day—walking the halls, greeting her old professors—but virtually, from London. Via Skype, students and professors at the university watched and listened as one of their alumna with an exceptionally strong character told her story.

Nancy had been invited to participate in a presentation of Los Otros Dreamers in Los Angeles, under the auspices of the CSUN Journalism Department. Jill and Nin had been invited to talk with students and professors about their project, and after reading aloud the introduction and some of the personal stories from the book, it was time to introduce Nancy. A self-assured young woman wearing a pink sweater appeared on the screen, her dark hair falling to her shoulders, and she talked to the audience.

> So, I am in the process of redefining myself and my relationship to the world. It no longer serves me to define myself as "Mexican," "American," "Undocumented," or "Deported." I prefer to see myself as a "Citizen of the World."

A month later, in May 2014, I had the opportunity to visit Nancy in London. She greeted me with a bright smile in her new city, the third she had lived in over the past five years. We hugged each other tightly, and practically as soon as she stepped back, Nancy began leading me around the streets of London. On the banks of the river Thames, right in front of the Parliament building, we started talking about what it meant to be a migrant, that abstract concept common to all nations, those that expel them and those that take them in; that identity that some study, while others condemn.

That evening we went out to dinner at a little restaurant in Piccadilly Circus. We talked about Los Angeles, the Dreamer activists in California and in the United States in general, and the #BringThemHome movement. We both knew that Nancy herself could have taken part in those actions, and if she had, she would probably be in Los Angeles right now. I asked her if she had thought about trying to come back through an academic channel now that she was an international student.

"The first two years I was always thinking about going back, but it got to a point where I closed that book myself and just focused on what was next. You can't always be thinking about what might have been or what might happen," she said emphatically, her eyes a bit misty. "Enough is enough. How much are you willing to risk your own personal dignity? How far are you willing to take the risk that they will reject you all over again?"

Then she told me about her near-term plans. In June she would finish classes and then travel to Mexico to work with Los Otros Dreamers.

"I think I can find a place there to put my knowledge to work," she said. "I have already talked to the people at Los Otros Dreamers and we have several projects. We're going to set up a support network for people who arrive, to help them get their academic certification in order, for example, and we're going to start working with the authorities, to try and eliminate some of the legal obstacles."

Before we said our good-byes, promising to meet again soon, in Mexico City next time, I asked Nancy one last question. Five years after having been expelled by the United States government, after starting a new life in Tijuana, after walking through the cities of London as part of a community of international students, with a plan now in place to embark on a career in Mexico City, what did she think of when she heard the word "home"?

"Los Angeles. Los Angeles will always be home."

As I write this, according to the countdown clock on Nancy's blog, she has 5.2 years to go before she can apply for a visa to come home.

APPENDIX

———◆———

THE DREAM ACT

THE DEVELOPMENT, RELIEF, AND EDUCATION for Alien Minors (DREAM) Act was first introduced in Congress as bill S. 1291 by Senator Richard Durbin on August 1, 2001. Since then, it has been reintroduced several times, with versions varying somewhat from the original. None of them has been passed into law.

The bill aims to amend legislation pertaining to immigration to allow undocumented immigrants the same access to higher education that citizens have, regardless of which state they live in. It would also grant the US attorney general authorization to cancel deportation proceedings and adjust the immigration status of those benefiting from the DREAM Act according to the requirements established within the law.

The most recent version of the DREAM Act, introduced by Senator Durbin in 2011 (S. 952), establishes the second objective with this text: "to authorize the cancellation of removal and adjustment of status of certain alien students who are long-term United States residents and who entered the United States as children and for other purposes."

To qualify for conditional permanent resident status under the DREAM Act, the applicant

- Must have continuously resided in the United States for five years immediately prior to the law's passage;
- Must have entered the country at fifteen years of age or younger;
- Must be a person of good moral character;

- Must have been accepted to an institution of higher learning, or have earned a high school diploma or its equivalent (GED);
- Must be younger than thirty-five years of age, as was specified in the first version of the DREAM Act. [Note: This requirement was modified to thirty-two years of age in a subsequent version and changed again to twenty-nine in the version S. 3992, debated in Congress in 2010. The most recent version, S. 952, raises the age requirement back to thirty-five];
- Cannot have been convicted of a crime.

As with all US immigration proceedings, applicants must follow a protocol including taking a physical exam, providing biometric data, and submitting to a background check. Once the law is enacted, the secretary of Homeland Security will have 180 days to publish regulations implementing the act.

After living in the United States as conditional permanent residents, applicants can become unconditional permanent residents if they meet the following requirements:

- Possess good moral character;
- Have no serious criminal convictions (all versions of the act include definitions of what constitutes a serious conviction);
- Have lived in the United States without interruption;
- Have earned a college diploma or have satisfactorily completed at least two years of a higher education program; or have served in the armed forces for at least two years.

The complete text of the original DREAM Act and subsequent versions can be found on the Library of Congress website:

http://beta.congress.gov/bill/107th-congress/senate-bill/1291.

ACKNOWLEDGMENTS

I CAME TO THIS COUNTRY TEN YEARS AGO, wanting to find out what was on the other side of the border. That search became a personal journey, with my partner and accomplice in this project, Diego Sedano, by my side. Without his faith and support, *Dreamers* would not have been possible.

I am forever grateful to Guillermo Osorno for his masterful patience, his faith in me, and his unwavering belief that the story of the Dreamers deserved to be told.

Thanks to Témoris Grecko, who called from Barcelona and ordered me to "drop everything else and write that book." To Gaspar Rivera-Salgado for his help in creating the structure when this project first began taking shape in my mind. To José Luis Benavides, Antonio Mejías-Rentas, Lilián López Camberos, Concepción Peralta, and Sandra Velázquez for their astute critiques of the manuscript. To Wilbert Torre for his interest and comments on the text. To my colleagues Diego Fonseca, Alex Sánchez, and Emiliano Ruiz Parra and to Silvia Rosas and Eliesheva Ramos for sharing their time and advice. To my mother, an enthusiastic reader of the first draft. To Memo, Rosal, and Alan, always there in every Dreamer I interviewed.

I gratefully acknowledge my colleagues at the Los Angeles newspaper *La Opinión*, my home for seven years and the place where I learned to see our migrants through the eyes of the heart.

The English-language edition of *Dreamers* would not have been possible without the support, enthusiasm, and faith of Diane Stockwell and Gayatri Patnaik. My heartfelt thanks to them and the team at Beacon Press: Helene Atwan, Tom Hallock, Melissa Nasson, Rachael Marks, and Travis Dagenais.

Also thanks to Pablo Martínez Lozada and the team at Editorial Océano in Mexico for the initial support given to this book with its publication in Spanish.

This book, telling an ever-evolving story, belongs to the young people who agreed to share their lives and their dreams with me. From the bottom of my heart I thank Mohammad Abdollahi, Santiago García-Leco, Benito Miller, Elioenaí Santos, Carlos Amador, Viridiana Hernández, Nancy Landa, Tania Chávez, Edith Belman, Jorge Luis Reséndez, José Ernesto Vázquez, Jorge Gutiérrez, Lizbeth Mateo, Claudia Amaro, Adriana Gil, and Sandra Jara. Thanks to Felipe Vargas, Alex Aldana, and the members of the #BringThemHome movement. To Jill Anderson, Nin Solís, and the members of Los Otros Dreamers. To the collective El Hormiguero in the San Fernando Valley. To Joaquín Luna's family, for opening the doors of their home and their memories to me, I cannot thank you enough.

SOURCES

INTRODUCTION: WE ARE ALL DREAMERS

Statistics on the undocumented workforce: Robert McNatt and Frank Benassi, "Econ 101 on Illegal Immigrants," *Bloomberg Businessweek*, http://www.businessweek.com, April 6, 2006.

Regarding figures on undocumented immigrants in the United States: Although by 2005 the standard number cited by analysts was twelve million, this number declined somewhat following the 2008 recession. A Pew Research Center study estimates that at the end of 2011, the number was 11.1 million: Jeffrey S. Passel and D'vera Cohn, "Unauthorized Immigrants: 11.1 Million in 2011," Pew Research Hispanic Trends Project, pewhispanic.org, December 6, 2012.

According to a report from the US Government Accountability Office, since fiscal year 1998, there has been an upward trend in the number of migrant border-crossing deaths annually, from 266 in 1998 to 472 in 2005, with some fluctuations over time. In 2012 the National Foundation for American Policy reported 477 deaths.

Regarding violence against migrants crossing Mexico, Amnesty International reports an estimate of twenty thousand people being kidnapped and or extorted on their way to the US. Other Mexican and international organizations have reported at least eighty thousand migrants disappeared in the last years of President Felipe Calderón's government.

In 2012 the Center for American Progress published a report on the economic impact of the passage of the DREAM Act. According to it, this would add a total of $329 billion to the economy by 2030, support the creation of 1.4 million new jobs, and generate more than $10 billion in increased revenue for the federal government.

CHAPTER ONE: A STUDENT IN NEED

Information on Deferred Action for Childhood Arrivals (DACA): Department of Homeland Security, "Deferred Action for Childhood Arrivals," http://www.dhs.gov/deferred-action-childhood-arrivals.

For information on the increase in deportations during Barack Obama's administration, see figures on deportations from Immigrations and Customs Enforcement (ICE): https://www.ice.gov/removal-statistics/. Figures on deportations from the Pew Center: Mark Hugo Lopez, Ana Gonzalez-Barrera, and Seth Motel, "As Deportation Levels Rise, Most Latinos Oppose Obama's Policy," Pew Research Hispanic Trends Project, http://www.pewhispanic.org, December 28, 2011.

CHAPTER TWO: UNDOCUMENTED AND UNAFRAID

Fernanda Marroquin's video testimonial before her arrest in Alabama: "Fernanda Marroquin," YouTube, http://www.youtube.com/watch?v= xhkNOgsDtVo, uploaded November 15, 2011.

The complete text of HB 56 from Alabama's state legislature can be found on the state government's website: Alabama Legislative Information System Online, http://alisondb.legislature.state.al.us/acas /ACASLoginMac.asp.

The complete text of SB 1070 from Arizona's state legislature can be found on the state government's website: "SB1070," Arizona State Legislature, http://azleg.gov/DocumentsForBill.asp?Bill_Number=sb1070.

On Barack Obama's meeting with Hispanic legislators, May 2011: "Casa Blanca y líderes hispanos del Congreso chocan sobre alivio a inmigrantes" (White House and Hispanic caucus clash over relief for immigrants), *Orlando Sentinel*, May 3, 2011, http://articles.orlandosentinel .com/2011-05-03/elsentinel/reforma-migratoria-previsin-20110503_1 _caucus-hispano-para-frenar-la-casa-blanca.

CHAPTER THREE: DREAM SELLER

Video of Senator Richard Durbin's presentation to Congress, September 20, 2011: "Pass the DREAM Act," YouTube, https://www.youtube.com /watch?v=oeG9qUqJbno&feature=youtu.be, uploaded September 28, 2011.

Excerpts from testimony before Congress about the DREAM Act and from letters to Senator Durbin were taken from the *Congressional Record*, September 20, 2011, http://www.gpo.gov/fdsys/pkg/CREC-2011 -09-20/content-detail.html.

Biographies of the Dreamers mentioned in this chapter—Mandeep Chahal, Fanny Martinez, and Tam Tran—were taken from speeches Senator Durbin gave in Congress and from testimonials from the Dreamers themselves, which can be found on Durbin's website, http://www.durbin

.senate.gov/public/index.cfm/hot-topics?ContentRecord_id=d17ca59b
-7420-441b-9ac2-2faf7549e9do. For Chahal, I also included informa-
tion published in "Not Legal, not Leaving" written by Jose Antonio Vargas and including quotes from thirty-six other undocumented youth, including Chahal, published in *Time*, June 25, 2012. Some information on
Tam Tran appeared in *Underground Undergrads: UCLA Undocumented
Immigrant Students Speak Out* and *Undocumented and Unafraid: Tam
Tran, Cinthya Felix, and the Immigrant Youth Movement*, edited by Kent
Wong et al., both published by the UCLA Center for Labor Research and
Education: http://books.labor.ucla.edu/p/55/undergroundundergrads and
http://books.labor.ucla.edu/p/79/undocumentedunafraid.

On Steven Camarota and the Center for Immigration Studies: "Steven A.
Camarota's Biography," Center for Immigration Studies, http://www.cis
.org/Camarota.

Predictions on the DREAM Act's economic impact by the Congressional
Budget Office: "Congressional Budget Office Cost Estimate," December
2, 2010, http://www.cbo.gov/sites/default/files/cbofiles/ftpdocs/119xx
/doc11991/s3992.pdf.

Data on wait times for immigration petitions for family members from
the National Immigration Forum: "Backgrounder: Immigration Back-
logs are Separating American Families," National Immigration Forum,
http://www.immigrationforum.org/images/uploads/FamilyBacklogBack
grounder.pdf.

The original *Los Angeles Times* article about Tam Tran, published in
2007, can be found at Teresa Watanabe, "Vietnamese Refugee Family
Finds Itself in Limbo," *Los Angeles Times*, October 19, 2007, http://
articles.latimes.com/2007/oct/19/local/me-deport19.

The complete Center for American Progress report on the economic benefits that will result from passing the DREAM Act: http://cdn.american
progress.org/wp-content/uploads/2012/09/statesProfiles_v10.pdf.

CHAPTER FOUR: BACK TO A STRANGE WORLD

The description of Nancy Landa's detention was based on interviews I
conducted with her in Tijuana, Mexico, and on her writings posted on
her blog *Mundo Citizen* (http://mundocitizen.com). Nancy provided me
with copies of her letter to Barack Obama and his response.

Data on deportations realized at San Ysidro: Andrew Becker and Agustin Armendariz, "California Border Crossing: San Ysidro Port of Entry Is
the Busiest Land Border in the World," *Huffington Post*, June 22, 2012,

http://www.huffingtonpost.com/2012/06/22/california-border-crossing
_n_1619067.html.

CHAPTER FIVE: CALIFORNIA DREAMING

I recreated some episodes from Gil Cedillo's life based on personal interviews with Gil and on information provided by people close to him and
involved with Southern California's Chicano movement.

On Meg Whitman's spending for her campaign for governor: Jack Chang,
"Meg Whitman's Grand Total: A Record $178.5 Million Spent," *Sacra-
mento Bee*, January 31, 2011, http://blogs.sacbee.com/capitolalertlatest/
2011/01/meg-whitmans-grand-total-a-rec.html.

I recreated the state legislature session approving the California DREAM
Act based on videos recorded by the State Assembly, transcriptions of the
speeches given, and reports published in the media.

General information on the California DREAM Act from the California
Dream Network: Justino Mora, "CA Dream Act Fact Sheet," November
30, 2011, http://www.cadreamnetwork.org/CA-Dream-Fact-Sheet.

Data on tuition costs in California from the California State University
Budget Office: "2012-13 Schedule of Systemwide Fees," http://www
.calstate.edu/budget/student-fees/mandatory-fees/1213-feeschedules.shtml;
and from the website California Colleges: "How Much Does College
Cost," https://secure.californiacolleges.edu/Financial_Aid_Planning
/Financial_Aid_101/how_much_does_college_cost.aspx.

On Dr. Alfredo Quinones, see an interview conducted by Dr. Sanjay
Gupta for CNN, "From Migrant Farm Worker to Surgeon," added October 5, 2010, http://www.cnn.com/video/#/video/health/2010/10/05/dnt
.gupta.dr.q.human.factor.cnn.

Other Sources

Stephanie Lewthwaite, *Race, Place and Reform in Mexican Los Angeles:
A Transnational Perspective, 1890–1940* (Tucson: University of Arizona
Press, 2009).

Javier Rodriguez, "Recordando a Bert Corona, lider de los derechos de
los trabajadores y migrantes en los EE.UU" (Remembering Bert Corona,
leader of the immigrant and labor rights in the US), *Latinas y Latinos
por el Cambio Social*, http://www.lfsc.org/sn_display1.php?row_ID=408.

A Chicano movement timeline from the Seattle Civil Rights and Labor
History Project: Oscar Rosales Castañeda, "Timeline: Movimiento from
1960–1985," http://depts.washington.edu/civilr/mecha_timeline.htm.

CHAPTER SIX: DREAMING IN ARIZONA

Information on Sheriff Joe Arpaio was taken from the Maricopa County Sheriff's Office at www.mcso.org/About/Sheriff.aspx and from Randy James, "Sheriff Joe Arpaio," *Time*, October 13, 2009, http://content .time.com/time/nation/article/0,8599,1929920,00.html.

Information from the Department of Justice on its legal actions against Arpaio: "Department of Justice Files Lawsuit in Arizona Against Maricopa County, Maricopa County Sheriff's Office, and Sheriff Joseph Arpaio," May 10, 2012, http://www.justice.gov/opa/pr/2012/May/12 -crt-602.html.

CHAPTER SEVEN: DYING FOR A DREAM

The description of Joaquin Luna's death was based on conversations with family members while I visited his home in Mission, Texas.

Data on potential beneficiaries of the Deferred Action for Childhood Arrivals program (DACA) from the report "Relief from Deportation: Demographic Profile of the DREAMers Potentially Eligible under the Deferred Action Policy" by the Migration Policy Institute: http://www .migrationpolicy.org/research/DACA-deferred-action-DREAMers.

CHAPTER EIGHT: DEFERRED ACTION

Information on the Deferred Action for Childhood Arrivals program (DACA): "Deferred Actions for Childhood Arrivals," United States Department of Homeland Security, http://www.dhs.gov/deferred-action -childhood-arrivals.

CHAPTER NINE: UNDOCUQUEERS

Demographic data on the San Fernando Valley used in this chapter and in the previous chapter came from the 2010 US Census, http://www .census.gov/2010census/.

Information about the amount of money generated by the pornography industry: "Internet Pornography Statistics," *Top Ten Reviews*, http:// internet-filter-review.toptenreviews.com/internet-pornography-statistics -pg2.html.

Information about the pornography industry in the San Fernando Valley: "Statistics," *Treasures*, http://iamatreasure.com/about-us/statistics /#sthash.nyisCiB4.Q6mX4815.dpbs; Madison Gray, "L.A. Mayor Signs Law Requiring Condoms in Porn Films," *Time*, January 25, 2012, http:// healthland.time.com/2012/01/25/l-a-mayor-signs-law-requiring condoms -in-porn-films/.

CHAPTER TEN: #BRINGTHEMHOME

Information on the Eloy Detention Center and Corrections Corporation of America can be found at the CCA website: http://cca.com.

The figure of 500,000 Dreamers who have returned to Mexico is from research by Jill Anderson, founder of Los Otros Dreamers: Jill Anderson, "From U.S. Immigration Detention Center to Transnational Call Center," *Voices of Mexico* 95 (2012): 87–91, http://www.revistascisan.unam.mx/Voices/pdfs/9517.pdf.

Video of Lizbeth Mateo recorded in Oaxaca: "Bring Them Home: Lizbeth Mateo Checking In from Oaxaca, Mexico," YouTube, https://www.youtube.com/watch?v=sDUyCszvQgk, uploaded July 17, 2013.

Further information on the Casas del Migrante of the Scalabrini International Migration Network can be found at http://www.migrante.com.mx.

EPILOGUE

Data on applicants to the DACA program through March 2014 can be found on the US Citizenship and Immigration Services website at http://www.uscis.gov/.

Jill Anderson and Nin Solís, *Los Otros Dreamers*, http://losotros dreamers.org.

Nancy Landa's blog, *Mundo Citizen*, can be found at http://mundocitizen.com.